"I DID IT MY WAY"

The Adversities & Triumphs of an Unlikely Community Banker

Memoirs of my blessed life and 60-year career

By J. Lamar Roberts

2Xalt
Viera

Copyright © 2019 by J. Lamar Roberts

All rights reserved. No part of this book may be used or reproduced by any means, graphic, electronic, or mechanical, including photocopying, recording, taping or by any information storage retrieval systems without the written permission of the publisher except in the case of brief quotations embodied in critical articles and reviews.

Published in Viera, FL by 2Xalt Press, an imprint of 2Xalt, Inc. Visit online at Press.2Xalt.com.

Contact the author at JLRoberts41@Yahoo.com

Because of the dynamic nature of the internet, any web addresses or links contained in this book may have changed since publication and may no longer be valid. The views expressed in this work are solely those of the author and do not necessarily reflect the view of the publisher, and the publisher hereby disclaims any responsibility for them.

Unless otherwise noted, Scripture quotations are from THE NEW KING JAMES VERSION, © 1979, 1980, 1982 by Thomas Nelson, Inc. Publishers.

Scripture quotations noted NASB are from the NEW AMERICAN STANDARD BIBLE®, © The Lockman Foundation 1960, 1962, 1963, 1968, 1971, 1972, 1973, 1975, 1977, 1988, 1995. Used by permission.

Scripture quotations noted NIV are from the HOLY BIBLE: NEW INTERNATIONAL VERSION, © 1973, 1978, 1984 BY International Bible Society. Used by permission of Zondervan Publishing House. All rights reserved.

Scripture quotations noted GNT are from the Good News Translation® (Today's English Version, Second Edition), © 1992 American Bible Society. All rights reserved.

ISBN: 978-0-9978157-8-8 (sc)

ISBN: 978-0-9978157-9-5 (e)

Printed in the United States of America.

Contents

Contents iii

PROLOGUE v

Chapter One – 1941 to 1959 1
    How Church Music Got Me into Banking. 1
    My Father was a Baptist Minister....................................... 2
    MY FATHER'S CALLING TO THE MINISTRY 5
    MOVING TO CHICAGO 7
    MOVING BACK TO GEORGIA 11

Chapter Two – 1959 to 1965 19
    MY FIRST BANK JOB 19

Chapter Three - 1965-1979 27
    Dixie County State Bank, Cross City, Fl 27

Chapter Four – 1979-1981 41
    FLORIDA NATIONAL BANK OF BREVARD 41

Chapter Five – 1981-1991 45
    First National Bank, Fort Walton Beach, FL 45

Chapter Six – Marrying Cindy 55

Chapter Seven – 1992-2009 59
    FIRST NATIONAL BANK OF PASCO 59
    Community and Banking Industry Involvement While in Pasco County 61

Chapter Eight – 2009-2011 71
    First National Bank of Central Florida................................ 71
    RMPI Consulting (Risk Management & Process Improvement Specialists).... 73

Chapter Nine – 2011-2019 75
    Fidelity Bank of Florida NA 75

Chapter Ten 103

It Is Not All About Me 103
MY GREATEST GIFTS, JOY, REGRETS, and HOPE 104
Appendix **105**
President's Message (Fidelity Bank's Web Page) 106
Articles written about me: 107
ARTICLES WRITTEN BY ME 115
PERSONALITY PROFILES 120
Resume 124
Business cards I had over my career. 128
GENEALOGY 129
MY FAVORITE CHRISTIAN ACRONYMS 132
SOME OF MY FAVORITE BIBLE VERSES 133
SOME OF MY FAVORITE QUOTES 134
SOME OF MY FAVORITE SONGS 136
ACTIVITIES, INVOLVEMENTS, INTEREST I HAVE HAD DURING MY LIFE 137

PROLOGUE

What are the chances that a boy, whose father was a "homeless person" and whose mother was the daughter of a "sharecropper" would become president of a bank at age 29?

Would the odds be even greater if he never made very good grades in school, never graduated from college and that his first Bank job was working as a part-time teller, making $1 per hour for a $12 million community bank?

Well, it happened! It happened to me!

In fact, after working as a teller for a few months, I became a loan clerk. When my boss was caught stealing $134,000, I was assigned a loan desk and told to start making installment (consumer) loans. I was 20 years old at the time.

I became a junior bank officer at age 21, department head at age 22, Assistant Vice President at age 23, head of operations for a Florida bank at age 24, Vice President at age 25, Board of Directors member at 26, President of the Rotary Club and Chamber of Commerce at age 27, Mayor and Municipal Judge at age 28 and President of a Bank at age 29.

During my career, I was locked in jail for driving a repossessed car with an expired tag, was sued personally by a bank stockholder for $25,000,000 and I had to turn over my bank keys, bank credit card and the bank's charter to the FDIC and the OCC when they closed a bank while I was its President.

Of course, there is a lot more to this story, such as becoming President of five other banks and Chairman of the Board of another. Several of those banks were either "turn around or crisis challenges" and three became high performers.

Being elected President of the Florida Bankers Association (FBA), as well as serving in leadership roles in the American Bankers Association and the Independent Community Bankers Association, were honors and opportunities that came with being an active and involved Community Banker. It did have its toll. During my year as President of the FBA, I had to take twelve days off to have quadruple heart bypass surgery.

More specific details and facts are included in this book. I hope it is a good read for all who pick it up and perhaps an example to some who might be questioning, "How can I deal with adversities and still accomplish my dreams."

Lamar Roberts

Chapter One – 1941 to 1959

HOW CHURCH MUSIC GOT ME INTO BANKING.

I trace the beginning of my banking career to a casual conversation I had after church services one Sunday. It was with Mr. Hewlett Grimes, the Chairman of the Board of Deacons for the church as well as the Chairman of the County Commission for Coweta County, Georgia, where we both lived. I was 18 years old, had graduated from Newnan High School the previous June and had just completed my first quarter as a freshman at West Georgia College in Carrollton, Georgia.

Mr. Grimes casually asked me "What type of work would you like to do for a career?" Without even thinking about it, I said, "I think I would like to work in a bank." He asked "Why?" I responded, "Their buildings are air-conditioned and I could wear a coat and tie every day." Nothing else was said until I saw him a couple of weeks later when he said, "I made an appointment for you tomorrow with Mr. Jay Smith, President of the Manufacturers National Bank. The bank was in Newnan, Georgia, thirty-eight miles southwest of Atlanta.

As I recall, I had only been in a bank a few times with my Dad and I did not even have a bank account. However, I kept the appointment and Mr. Jay, as everyone called him, offered me a part-time teller job working Friday afternoons and Saturday mornings for $1 per hour. I had a similar job working for a grocery store, running a cash register. It also paid $1 per hour. Even though it was a reduction in my income and fewer hours to work at the bank, I took the job. That was the beginning of what was to become my sixty-year career in banking.

The name of this chapter implies that church music got me into banking. At the time of my conversation with Mr. Grimes, I was also employed at the Providence Baptist Church. My part-time job with the church was as their Music Director. It paid $60 per month.

I had been involved in music since the seventh grade when I joined the school band and learned to play the school-owned Sousaphone (tuba). My father wanted my brother, Bill, and me both to play in the band but he could only afford to buy one instrument, a flute for my younger brother.

That began my interest in music. Eventually, my father sold Bible Story Books in order to buy me a trombone. I learned to play it, a baritone, and I taught myself how to play a few hymns on the piano. I was also a member of the school's chorus and always sung in Boys Quartets. All of that led to my involvement in church music.

When I was a senior at Newnan High School, I was hired by two "part-time" Baptist churches to organize, train and lead their choirs as well as their congregational singing. I was paid an average of $25 per week. These churches were referred to as "part-time churches" because they only had services every other Sunday. That meant that I worked at one church on the 1st and 3rd Sunday of each month and at the other church on the 2nd and 4th Sundays. I also conducted choir practices every Tuesday and Thursday nights.

During the summer months or during the Christmas season, I would work for other churches either leading the music for their revivals or producing their Christmas pageants. I usually was paid $50 to $100 for my services at these events. However, one small church decided to take up an offering for the Minister and the Music Director giving the Minister all the currency and the music guy, me, all the change. I believe I received about $28.67 for that one week's work.

MY FATHER WAS A BAPTIST MINISTER.

You will remember that I mentioned in the prelude to this book that my father was a "homeless" person and now I am telling you that he was a "preacher." Both are true, one is how he started his adult life; the other became his career.

My Father, Elihu Dee Robert, was born in Manatee, Florida, in 1907. That is where his Father had "homesteaded." In fact, the deed to his homesteaded property indicates that it was signed by President Woodrow Wilson years later. Sometime between my Father's birth, and when he turned 16, his family moved to Broken Bow, Oklahoma, where my grandfather apparently homesteaded another farm. It was there that my Father's Mother died at an early age. My father had a brother named Jehu and two sisters. Their names were Bobbie and Johnnie.

I did not learn until my Father's death, in 1972, at age 65, about the years he was a homeless person. It was then my mother told me that he had dropped out of school when he was in the seventh grade. At age sixteen, he ran away from home. That was the same year his mother died. For the next ten years, he was a "train hopping, field sleeping hobo" traveling all over the country as a migrate worker, truck driver or any other job he could find.

Somehow, he arrived in Georgia when he was about twenty-six years of age. That is where he met my Mother. They were both working in a textile mill in Hogansville. My Mother, Edna Estelle Thompson, was born in Heard County, Georgia in 1912. Her father, Lonnie Thompson, and my Grandmother, Rose, were sharecroppers. Sharecroppers did not own their farms. They worked for farm owners and received a "share" of the farm's production as their pay. Most sharecroppers were, like my grandparents, very poor.

The largest crops they grew were corn and cotton. In my Mother's first book, "Experiences That Live," she tells about how her family lived off the land. They ate what they grew in their gardens, the eggs their chickens produced, and they drank the milk the cows gave. Their pork meat came from the pigs they raised, killed and salted to preserve in their "smokehouse." A smokehouse was a small barn where fresh-killed meat hung to cure. The meat was heavily salted to preserve it for the months before it was consumed.

Some other necessities were bartered for from the "rolling store, a truck that came down the dirt country roads each week. Bartered means they exchanged eggs or produce they had for items they needed but did not have the cash to buy. My Mother also recounted in her book that her Father would go through a harsh winter with only one $5 bill folded up in his overalls (farmer's work pants with a bib). That cash was only spent on emergencies.

1 The picture on the left is my Father, Elihu Dee Roberts, in about 1932. He was working at Bibb Manufacturing Company in Columbus, GA. The picture on the right is my parents, Elihu Dee Roberts and Edna Estelle Roberts. It was made in 1942 when I was one year old.

2 My parents built this home in 1940. I was born in the front bedroom. The house was on Corinth Road near Hogansville, GA.

MY FATHER'S CALLING TO THE MINISTRY

My parents were married in April 1934, and my brother Lonnie Dee was born in September 1935. He was named for his two grandfathers. A few years later, my parents were able to buy fifty acres of land and an adjoining lot near Hogansville GA. On it, they built a new home, complete with an "outhouse", our outdoor toilet. It was in the front bedroom of that house where I was born, July 21, 1941, four and one-half months before the Japanese bombed Pearl Harbor. I was named Lamar after my Mother's former Sunday School teacher's baby. When my mother was a preteen, while rocking the baby, she said that if she ever had a son she would name him Lamar, that baby's name. That baby grew up to be a successful Attorney and Judge. I met him years later.

3   This is a copy of my birth certificate. Notice the job descriptions for each of my parents ("Twister Tender" and "Warper Creeler").

MOVING TO CHICAGO

My parents lived on a tight budget trying to raise two young boys and make house payments on mill worker's wages. That led to my Father getting very upset when he came home one day to learn that my Mother had bought a Bible Storybook from a door-to-door salesman. The price of the book was $5. She had agreed to make payments of $1 per week. My Father's frustrated exclamation was, "If I have to pay for that book, I will read it!"

He did and immediately began attending church regularly. It was not long before he decided he had been "called to be a minister" and that he had to "preach or bust." One of the few schools accepting students training for the ministry, who only had a seventh-grade education, was Moody Bible Institute in Chicago IL.

Therefore, my Father sold our home, our car, and our furniture quit his job and took a passenger train to Chicago. My mother, older brother and I stayed in Hogansville, Ga to live in a house owned by the textile mill where she worked. These houses were located near the mill in a subdivision called the Mill Village and, therefore, was within walking distance of the mill. However, both the husband and the wife had to work in the textile mill for the family to qualify for a house. That resulted in my mother, brother and me moving into a converted chicken house in an area called "Little Mexico." I was eighteen months old.

About six months later, my Father was able to have the three of us join him in Chicago. There the four of us lived in a rented one-bedroom apartment that would only accommodate a bunk bed. My brother and I slept on the top bunk and our parents slept on the bottom. Thus my youngest brother, William Eugene (Billy), was conceived.

To support the growing family, my father decided he would have to stop going to school fulltime and instead get a full time job and attend school at night. My mother was able to locate a low-cost clinic to care for her before my brother was born. On the way to her first visit to the clinic, she stopped by the Post Office. An envelope was in our mail addressed to her. It contained six dollars and the scripture verse, Philippians 4:6 "Don't worry about anything, instead, pray about everything; tell God your needs and don't forget to thank Him for His answers." There was no name on the paper. It was years later before my parents learned that the note and money were from another couple who were attending Moody and who knew about my parents' situation. Later that couple became Missionaries to Africa. I have a picture of them with other memorabilia from that era.

The woman at the clinic took my mother's information about the family's living conditions and income. She then asked, with tears in her eyes, "Mrs. Roberts, are you telling me that a family of four has survived on this income in Chicago for the past six months?" My mother answered "Yes." The women then said, "Do you know that you are required to pay a $6 fee for your first visit here?" My mother then reached into her purse for the $6 dollars she had just received in the mail. Obviously, God works in mysterious ways, His wonders to perform!

Billy, my youngest brother, was born in June 1944 and named by my older brother, Lonnie. He asked that his baby brother be called "Billy" after the then famous evangelist, Billy Sunday. His legal name was William Eugene.

While the five of us were living in the two-room apartment, all three of the boys came down with measles. Then, just as we were getting better, our father came down with a very severe case. His was so bad that the doctor would not allow him to attend his classes at Moody or go to work. That meant we had no income.

My mother later told the family of an event that happened during those dark and trying times. She said the owner of the apartment where the five of us were living, walked by the back door one Saturday and asked my older brother and me how the family was doing. I told the woman about our dad's illness, him not being able to go to work or go to classes and that we had no money and no food. The next day she knocked on our door and presented my mother a large basket of food. She expressed concern about our situation and said not to worry about the rent and that she would be providing us groceries until my father was well and able to go back to work. Prayers were answered!

Sometime later, my father accepted a job to manage a Christian Mission. It was in a large three-story building complete with a four-room furnished apartment for the manager and his family.

While living at the mission, Daddy received a check for the equity in the house he had sold in Georgia when he moved to Chicago. With that money, we were able to buy furniture and rent a five-room apartment across the street from Moody Bible Institute.

Shortly after moving into this apartment Billy, the baby developed spinal meningitis and nearly died. About a year later, he had such a bad reaction to mosquito bites that he was hospitalized again. Both of these conditions affected him the rest of his life, but not bad enough to keep him from being drafted. Instead of going into the army, he joined the Air Force where he became an Air Traffic Controller.

As we moved into our new apartment, Daddy took a job at The Derby Laundry, an industrial laundry located in a very large four-story building within walking distance of our new apartment. His first job there was shoveling coal in the boiler room located in the basement of the building. This was a very hot, physically hard job. However, as his schooling progressed, so did his position with the laundry. Eventually, he had a private office on the top floor with the job titles of Human Resource Officer and Industrial Chaplain.

For many years, I have kept a framed copy of a 1946 Chicago newspaper article with the headline "Laundry That Cleanses Employees' Souls." It includes a picture of my father leading a religious meeting of the employees and quotes him as saying "I prefer hiring believers or those I think I can convert and I will not employ avowed scoffers."

4 This picture is of my father interviewing a job applicant at the laundry. Notice the sign on the wall, the cross, and Bible on the desk

While living at 819 North Wells Street in Chicago, I turned six years old and had to begin attending school. The local public school was integrated and my parents, being from the south, did not think that was an appropriate place for me to attend school. The only other option was a Lutheran Parochial School. My father was studying to be a Baptist minister, not a Lutheran Priest. Therefore, he had to choose between my brother and me attending school with minorities or the Lutherans. I still have my Lutheran Catechism book.

5 This picture on the left is of me when I was about three years old, 1944. I was sitting outside the Mission in Chicago that my father managed. The picture on the right is of our family in 1947, the year I started first grade. It includes my mother, father, older brother Lonnie on the left and younger brother Billy on the right. I am standing in the middle.

MOVING BACK TO GEORGIA

In 1949, my father graduated from Moody Bible Institute in Chicago and announced to the family that he was resigning his job at the laundry and that we were moving back to Georgia. He explained that it had always been his plan to be a Baptist Minister in the area where we had lived in Georgia. That is where we had a lot of family and friends.

I was in the second grade when he sold our furniture and the five of us boarded a passenger train for Georgia with only our luggage. We moved into a three-room unpainted, clapboard, tin-roofed tenant house on a farm owned by my uncle. It was near Grantville, GA. The house built on rock pillars had a well in the front yard and an outhouse in the back yard. We were allowed to live there rent-free since neither my mother nor my father had a job. I was told that we were the first white people to ever live in this house.

6 This is a picture of the tenant house where we lived. That is my Mother, my younger brother, and me dressed in our "Sunday go to meeting" clothes.

With the money they had from selling our furniture in Chicago, they bought three beds, mattresses and springs, a kitchen table, four chairs and a bench for Billy and me to sit on at the table. They also bought a kerosene stove, an icebox, and a 1939 two-door Chevrolet.

We nailed thin plywood, from discarded shipping boxes to the studs inside the house for the interior walls. There were none when we got there. Neither was there ever any insulation and there was only one fireplace for heat. Therefore, we boys had to cut wood to burn in the fireplace, take out the ashes and paint the hearth with "white mud" which we gathered from a creek bottom.

We strung electric wires from the rafters for the three ceiling lights, one for each room. A lot of our food came from the farm, including milk from the farm cows, and vegetables from our garden as well as eggs from the chickens that ran loose around the yard. My maternal grandparents lived in the farms "big house" and worked on the farm. An ice wagon would come to each home every week. From it, we would buy a block of ice for the icebox where we kept the food that needed to remain cold. We did not own a refrigerator.

Daddy became the Pastor of two part-time churches (they only had services every other Sunday) and mother went back to work in the textile mill. She worked on the second shift, two p.m. to 10 p.m. and, therefore; she did not get home until about midnight. That resulted in her being gone when we got home from school, we were asleep when she got home from work and she was still asleep when we left for school. We only saw her on weekends. At that time, I was eight years old; Billy was five and Lonnie, eleven.

It was during a summer Church Revival at Providence Baptist Church in Troup County, GA, in 1950, that I accepted Jesus Christ as my personal Savior, asked for forgiveness of my sins and was baptized in a nearby farm pond. The pond was not far from the house where I was born. I was nine years old and the first person my Father ever baptized. One of my prized possessions is this black and white photograph of the occasion.

7 *My baptism in a farm pond near Hogansville, GA*

Mother referred to Daddy as the "soul winner" and Daddy referred to Mother as the "breadwinner." She made more money working in the mill than he earned as a pastor. To my knowledge, my father never made over $100 a week in his life.

Within a year or so, we moved to an upstairs, four-room apartment with an inside bathroom, in Grantville GA. There we three boys could walk to school instead of riding the school bus and Mother could more easily carpool to the textile mill in Hogansville, six miles down the road. By that time, my father could afford to buy a gas stove, gas heaters, a refrigerator and eventually a television. We even got a newer car by trading our 1939 Chevrolet for a 1947 Chevrolet.

When I was in the fourth grade, I started selling the local newspaper door to door. The price was 10 cents. I received 5 cents for each sale. When I was in the fifth grade, I got a job working at a grocery store on Friday afternoons and Saturdays, delivering groceries by riding a bike. My earnings were 75 cents for working four hours on Friday afternoon and $2.50 for fifteen hours on Saturday.

Since I was not tall enough to ride the special bike the store provided, which had an oversized basket, I bought myself a smaller bike, which was financed by my employer. I was 10 years old. I paid them $1 per week out of the $3.25 cents I earned. Each Monday I would buy $1 of savings stamps, and when they totaled $18.75, I would exchange the stamps for a $25 war savings bond. Now they are called E Bonds. These were my first business transactions, financing a bike and buying savings bonds.

I saved those bonds until I was a senior in High School. At that time, I was working for churches in their music ministry. My mother, the church pianist, needed a piano at our home to practice the music I had selected. Therefore, I cashed in my bonds and bought her a rebuilt piano.

MOVING TO FRANKLIN, GA - 1953

We moved to Franklin, GA, in Heard County, not far from Grantville, when I was in the seventh grade. There, my Dad was the Pastor of the First Baptist Church. Since moving back to GA in 1949, he had been attending night school classes offered by Mercer University. In 1956, he graduated from Mercer and then he got his General Education Diploma, GED, the equivalent of a High School Diploma.

This church had a Baptist Training Union (BTU). It was similar to but in addition to, Sunday School. As I recall the classes were on Sunday evenings and were only for young people. Each person was given a monthly booklet, which contained various short lessons. The lessons were about the Church, the Bible or Christian life. Each of us was assigned a different lesson to study and then we stood in front of the class to tell those present the essence of the lesson without reading it to them. This gave us the opportunity, and requirement, to make a short presentation, talk or speech. I realized later in life that this training greatly helped me in becoming comfortable making presentations to small or large groups.

MOVING TO REBECCA, GA - 1955

When I was in the 9th grade, we moved to Rebecca, GA, where my father was the Pastor of the Rebecca Baptist Church. While living there, I worked as a janitor and painter for the church and I worked for several farmers. On the farms, I "strung" tobacco, hauled watermelons and cantaloupes, plowed peanut fields, sacked peanuts on a peanut combine and picked cotton. The pay for picking cotton was $3 per one hundred pounds picked. Unfortunately, I could not even pick 100 lbs.in a day so I only made about $2 per day.

Rebecca, GA, in Turner County, is in the southern part of Georgia. The town was so small that it only had two churches, two grocery stores, two bars, and one drug store. The county seat of Turner County, Ashburn, was about twelve miles west of Rebecca. While living in Rebecca, I rode a school bus each day to attend Ashburn High School. When I was in the 11th grade, I attended the new Turner County High School.

It was while living in South Georgia that I began driving the family car, a 1953 Chevrolet. I do not remember how I learned to drive. Back then, most young people drove farm vehicles, either tractors or trucks, so that is probably what I drove first. I did take Drivers Education in the 10th grade. The car, furnished, by a local car dealer, was a new 1956 Chevrolet, with a 6-cylinder engine, and a straight stick transmission. That means the transmission was not automatic so the driver had to push in a floor pedal (clutch) to change the gears. I already was driving the family car so there was nothing to learn about driving the car, just the rules of the road.

Even though I do not remember how I learned to drive, I do remember that I did not take a test to get my driver's license. We lived about 25 miles from the nearest Highway Patrol Station where everyone was supposed to go to be tested. That was inconvenient, so a neighbor, who was a state trooper, took my driver's education certificate to his station and brought me back my license. That was one of the advantages of living in a small town and knowing a friendly trooper.

I remember a night when my younger brother, Billy, and I were at home alone. Our parents were out with another couple, leaving our family car at home with the key in it. The key was always left in the ignition regardless of where it was parked, just as the doors on our home were never locked. Everyone trusted everybody.

Billy and I knew that there was a dance party for young people not far from our house but we were not allowed to attend. As "preacher kids" we could not dance, play cards, attend movies, shoot pool or play pinball machines. We decided that since we could not attend the dance we could at least "borrow" the car and drive by to see how much fun our friends were having. However, as I drove by I took my eyes off the road to look in the dance hall and yes, you guessed it, I ran into the ditch. I do not recall any major damage to the car, but I cannot say the same for Billy and me. I was about thirteen years old.

However, I was allowed to drive the family car even before I got my license. In fact, I believe I was either fourteen or fifteen when my Dad allowed me to use it for my first date. It was to take my girlfriend to a Saturday afternoon swimming party at the only pool in town.

He told me that he knew how far it was to her house and that I was not to go anywhere else. Since I thought we might be going elsewhere, after getting out of sight of our home, I stopped the car and disconnected the odometer. As it turned out, we did not go anywhere else and I was nearly back home when I realized I had not recorded any miles on the odometer. To correct this, I once again stopped the car, reconnected the odometer, and retraced my trip to my girlfriend's home and to the party site before returning home with the correct miles recorded.

Another night, when I had been allowed to take the car on a date, I lost control of it coming down a hill and ran into a swamp. I had to climb out of the window since water would not let me open the door. I walked a few miles home and told my Dad I had car trouble. He said we would see about it in the morning. I had to skip school that day and go with Dad to ask a farmer to pull the car out of the swamp. The dents in the bumper and body of the car were never repaired.

One day my Dad told me that I had been observed passing one of the church members while driving eighty-five miles an hour. I told him that could not be true since our 1953 Chevrolet would only go eighty. I was fortunate to receive only a scolding for this infraction of the rules.

I was concerned that there might be more consequences since he did take my driving privilege away for six weeks one time when I made an "F" in Algebra. It is amazing how long six weeks is when you are a teenager with a want and need to get back behind the wheel.

A few years later, we had an 1953 Ford V8 that would go faster than 80 miles an hour. I know because one time I was driving faster than that when I blew a rod in the car's engine.

MOVING TO ASHBURN, GA - 1957

When I was going into the eleventh grade, we moved to Ashburn GA, the county seat of Turner County. There I could walk to school. I played the trombone in the band, sang in the chorus and in the boy's quartet. I also sang in a men's quartet at First Baptist Church.

We were living in Ashburn when I got my first "real" job. It was working part-time in the butcher shop of a grocery store. My pay was $0.75 per hour. That was better than the $0.50 an hour I was making doing odd jobs around town. Unfortunately, after a few months of working in the grocery store, the economy went into a recession and my position was eliminated.

It was about that time that my father was "called" (offered the job) to be the minister at two part-time churches in the Newnan, GA area. This was when I was in the middle of the eleventh grade and very involved in various music programs. A local insurance agent and his wife, Mr., and Mrs. John Johnson asked my parents to allow me to live with them until the end of that school year. That was a unique experience for me. My Mother sent me $3 per week for my school lunches and pocket money. Mr. Johnson actually allowed me to use his car to take my girlfriend on a date. Obviously, he did not know of my driving record.

MOVING TO NEWNAN, GA - 1958

I moved to Newnan, GA, the summer before I entered the twelfth grade at Newnan High School. This was a much better school than those I had attended in South Georgia. They required an additional math course and an additional science class for me to graduate. I had only had one math course, first-year algebra, and I had to take it twice to get a passing grade. To get the other math credit, the school allowed me to take General Math, a ninth-grade class.

The only science course that was available for me to take was Physics and I was very unprepared to take it. Not only had I not had second-year algebra, I had not taken trigonometry or calculus. However, the Physics teacher needed one more person for the minimum number students required for the class. He told me, "If you will agree to attend all the classes and watch a physics class offered on TV daily at 6 AM, I will guarantee you will make at least "D" in the class." That would allow me to graduate. I agreed and did what he required, he kept his word and I graduated in June 1959. I saw him fifty years later at our class reunion and ask if he remembered our deal. He smiled and said, "Yes I do."

During my senior year in High School, I got a part-time job working at a local chain grocery store. My first job there, once again, was in the meat department, cutting up chickens and grinding hamburger meat. My pay was $0.90 per hour. Later, I transferred to the front of the store to bag groceries. All grocery carts had numbers on the front of them. After customers paid their bill, the "sack boys" would give them a piece of paper with the number of their grocery carts on it and then we would roll their cart to the sidewalk outside the store. Customers would drive to the front of the store, give us the number of their carts, and we would load their groceries into their cars.

It was not long before I was operating a cash register. My pay was then increased to $1 per hour.

During my senior year in High School, I also began working part time jobs as the Music Director for various churches. As mentioned earlier, this paid about $25 per week. The summer after I graduated, I met a beautiful young girl, Joyce Tidwell, who was an accomplished pianist and a trained, talented vocalist. This was the summer after she had completed the tenth grade. Her father, Weston Tidwell, was a mill worker and the Mayor of the small town where they lived, Moreland, GA. We started dating soon after we met.

Chapter Two – 1959 to 1965

In September 1959, I moved into a dormitory on the West Georgia College campus in Carrollton, GA. Carrollton was about twenty-five miles west of Newnan. My Dad wanted me to have the experience of living in a dorm even though I had to come back to Newnan each Tuesday and Thursday nights to conduct choir practices. I also came home every weekend to work at the grocery store. Sundays I conducted church music programs in the mornings and evenings.

To make all these commutes, my Dad borrowed my grandparent's life savings, $200, and bought me a used 1950 Plymouth, 6-cylinder, with a straight stick transmission. I repaid my grandparents with my first Christmas bonus from the Bank. It was one month's salary, which happened to be, $200. While attending West Georgia College, I traded the Plymouth for a 1954 Dodge with a V8 engine and an automatic transmission.

My work and school schedule did not leave much time for dating. Therefore, I proposed to Joyce, Easter weekend, in 1960. She was in the eleventh grade. We married in June 1961 two weeks after she graduated from high school. On our honeymoon trip to Gatlinburg, Tennessee, we celebrated with a bottle of Ginger Ale. It was not until our first vacation to New Orleans the next year that we both had our first taste of a drink containing alcohol. BIG MISTAKE! This contributed to her early death.

MY FIRST BANK JOB

February 1960, The Manufacturers National Bank in Newnan offered me a part-time teller job. It paid $1 per hour, the same amount I earned at the grocery store. That summer I worked full-time at the bank, and when I was about to register for my second year at West Georgia College, the bank offered me a full-time job paying $200 per month. The job was for five and one-half days per week. They agreed for me to leave a little early on Monday, Wednesday and Friday afternoons so I could commute to Georgia State College in Atlanta to attend evening classes. Atlanta was about 40 miles north of Newnan. The bank also agreed to pay for all of my tuition and book expenses. I made that commute for about three years.

My mother kidded me about working seven days a week but not making any money between midnight and six a.m. About that time one of the Bank Directors, the owner of a local manufacturing company, died. His widow was afraid to stay in their mansion at night by herself so the bank president asked if I would agree to sleep at her home for $5 per night. That meant that I was then making money seven days a week nearly twenty-four hours per day.

I never saw the widow during the time I was in the house. I was to be there by midnight and ring the doorbell as I entered her home to let her know that I had arrived. My bedroom was next to hers and there was a phone by my bed in the event she needed me. She never called but she left me a check each Friday night. I gave up that job when I got married in June 1962.

During this same time, I accepted an additional job as Treasurer of the local Country Club. My duties were to bill and collect the members' dues each month. I was paid $25 per month and they waived my membership dues.

8 I bought this house in 1961 when I was nineteen years of age. It was in LaGrange Heights Subdivision, at 52 Bailey Drive, Newnan, GA.

Joyce and I married two weeks after she graduated from High School. She was seventeen and I was nineteen. I bought her a new 1960 Plymouth Valiant for $2,000. It had a push-button transmission on the left side of the dash. Our second car was a used 1950 Desoto which I drove to work at the bank.

I had purchased a two-bedroom, one-bath brick home for $5,000 about six months before the wedding. The seller of the house sold us all of his furniture for $100 and I paid $25 for a used black and white television. When the bank remodeled their drive-in teller, they gave me an old window air conditioner, which I had installed, in our bedroom. I had to borrow the $500 down payment to buy the house from the bank where I was working.

In 1963, we built a new, all-electric, three-bedroom, two-bath, two-car garage home on a one-acre lot in a subdivision just outside the Newnan city limits. Little did I know that we would live there less than two years. That new home cost $14,000 plus the lot, which I acquired with the equity in our first home.

When I started my full-time job at the Bank, they assigned me to the Loan Administration Department where I worked as a clerk. My job was to accept and post loan payments and process new loans. It was while I was in this department that it was determined that my boss had embezzled about $132,000. They fired him and he went to jail. He was to have been the best man at our wedding that summer. However, I never saw or heard from him after his arrest.

While working as a loan clerk the bank president asked me to do some collecting of past-due loan payments. This meant I would go to the home of customers (very few had telephones), who were delinquent on their payments and try to collect the money they owed. I asked the President how to get them to pay. He said, first you try to talk them out of the payment, if that does not work, then try to trick them into paying and if all else fails, cuss them into paying. I do not recall ever having to cuss.

Shortly after my supervisor was caught embezzling from, Mr. Jay, the Bank's President approached my workstation and asked if I thought I could make loans. I told him that I had watched the loan officers and I was sure I could. I was twenty years old and thought I could do anything anyone else could do. He assigned me a desk and told me to interview installment loan customers (now referred to as consumer loans) and, if I thought the loan could be approved, I was to take it to an officer of the bank to see if they would initial the loan showing they agreed with my decision. He explained they he could not make me an officer because I was not of legal age. After a few months, I just started initialing the loans I made and no one ever questioned my authority to do so.

The bank had no written loan policies, no application forms, no job descriptions, no credit files and was not even a member of the credit bureau. To decide on approving a loan request, we just talked to customers, looked them in the eye, checked to see if they had borrowed from the bank before, and if so, did they pay on time. It was truly character and collateral-based lending.

We also had to determine the value of the collateral, usually cars, but sometimes real estate. For cars, we used the National Automobile Dealers Association (NADA) book, which listed all makes and models of cars and indicated their average market value and loan value. If the collateral was real estate, we would drive by the house and make a guess at its value. I made loans for nearly twenty years before we used outside appraisers or even got title insurance. Instead of a title policy we would get an Attorney's Letter of Opinion stating the bank had a good first lien. It was also about twenty years before I foreclosed on a real estate mortgage and that was not on a loan that I had approved.

I did repossess many cars. I think having that experience helped me be a more cautious loan officer. There were a few Friday nights that I made collection calls to homes in the more destitute areas of Atlanta. On those few occasions, I carried a pearl-handled pistol tucked into my belt. Of course, I never had to touch it. My home county, Coweta, had issued me a "Pistol Totters Permit" similar to the Concealed Weapons License that is issued today. My father had to sign a bond for me to get the permit.

Once I had to repossess a car from an unemployed preacher. He got very upset with me and said, "You will answer on judgment day for taking my car." As he was saying that, I started driving the Renault down the hill in front of his apartment. It was only then that I realized that the brakes would not work and, apparently, that day was going to be my "judgment day." Fortunately, I was able to downshift the gears, slow the car, make the turn ahead of me and then curb the car to get it stopped. I do not think I ever repossessed another car from a Preacher.

One morning a couple approached my desk very hurriedly, sat down and said they needed a $200 loan fast because they were on the way to the hospital for the birth of their child. I noticed that she was about nine and one-half months pregnant and I quickly determined that they did not qualify for the loan. About that time, she let out a long moan and grabbed her large abdomen.

It became apparent that the child was going to be born in the bank, at my desk, if I did not get them out immediately. I grabbed a blank unsecured note form, typed it out, had them sign it, gave them the cash and hurried them on their way. A few weeks later, when they returned to pay the loan in full, I learned that the baby was born that afternoon.

In the summer of 1963, my wife and I were vacationing on Jekyll Island, GA. While there, the bank called to say that the Exchange Bank in Tampa, FL. had repossessed a car I had financed. The borrower had defaulted and skipped town. However, it had been "skip traced" to Tampa and the Exchange Bank had repossessed it for me. It was customary at that time for banks to repossess cars for other banks as a courtesy. The bank officer that called me from The Manufacturers National Bank suggested that my wife and I drive over to Tallahassee FL, fly to Tampa and drive the car back to Newnan. This was an adventure for us since we had never flown in an airplane.

July 3, 1963, as we were driving the repossessed car back to Tallahassee, a Florida State Trooper stopped me in Levy County, FL. The trooper said the car I was driving had an expired tax and he asked for the registration. I told him I did not have the car's registration and explained that I was a banker returning a repossessed car to my bank in Georgia.

He apparently did not believe me because he instructed me to follow him. I did not realize that we were going to the Sheriff's Office in Bronson FL. There I explained the situation again and told them that if I could use their phone to make a collect call to the bank in Newnan, they could vouch for me, purchase a tag and have the tag agent confirm that to the Deputy.

That seemed to satisfy them. However, after I hung up the phone, they said I could wait upstairs. It was then, as I was walking up the iron stairs with a deputy behind me, that I realized I was being locked in jail. He placed me in a large cell with six other criminals. My wife was waiting for me in the car and no one would tell her where I was.

A couple of hours later, a deputy took me before the County Judge. He said, "You have been charged with driving a car with an expired tag. How do you plead?" I said I was guilty but that I would like to explain. He said that since I pled guilty, he would have to fine me $25. I told him that was all the cash I had on me and that I needed it to get back to Georgia. He then said he would suspend my sentence because the Sheriff of Coweta County, GA, where my bank was located, had called him and vouched for me.

The Judge then gave me a letter explaining my circumstances and told me I could show it to any other officer who might stop me before I got back to Newnan. I thanked him profusely. However, I was so upset I vowed never to return to Florida. Little did I know that within three years we would be living in the adjoining county and three years after we moved there, I would be a Municipal Judge sending people to jail.

In 1962, at the age of twenty-one, I was promoted to Assistant Cashier, a junior officer position at that time. The following year I became manager of the Installment Loan Department and at twenty-three, promoted to Assistant Vice President.

The Bank in Newnan had been giving me raises from my beginning salary of $2400 per year. They were small raises but one year the bank's new Comptroller told the Bank President that my salary would have to be at least $100 per week or they would have to start paying me over-time. They immediately increased my salary to $400 per month. The Controller then told the president that was only $4,800 per year and to meet the wage and salary laws I would have to be paid $5,200. Therefore, I received another $400 increase. When I was promoted to Assistant Vice President in January 1965, they increased my annual salary to $6,000.

During this time, I worked five and one-half days a week at the bank, worked for two churches in their music ministries Tuesday and Thursday nights as well as Sundays and attended Georgia State College in Atlanta on Monday, Wednesday and Friday nights.

While continuing to do all of that, in 1962, to further my career and education, the bank agreed to send me to the new three-year Georgia School of Banking at the University of Georgia in Athens. I would attend two-week sessions each summer for the three years and submit six projects, (case studies) one each month, to the school between sessions. One of our classes was public speaking. The person with the best speech, as determined by the professor, was to be the speaker at the commencement ceremony. In my senior year, 1964, I made that speech and was given a trophy as shown in the picture below.

9 Picture of me and others who spoke at the Graduation Ceremony, Georgia School of Banking, University of Georgia, June 1964.

It was during one of these summer sessions that I observed my first "panty raid" on a girl's dorm. Apparently, that was not an unusual occurrence. All it amounted to was boys standing outside the girl's dormitory and the girls throwing their panties out the window.

That summer I also witnessed a Ku Klux Klan (KKK) rally. The KKK was a white supremacy group that organized in the south after the civil war. The group that I saw did nothing but walk back and forth on the sidewalk in front of the Varsity Restaurant. The Klan consisted of white men dressed in white robes and wearing a white hood. Later, I did see the Klan burn a cross in the front yard of a house. This despicable practice was usually done to let the residents know that the Klan did not approve of them and as a warning that the Klan might return to do them harm.

After graduating from The Georgia School of Banking in 1964, I told the bank that I now wanted to attend the three-year School of Banking of the South at Louisiana State University in Baton Rouge, Louisiana. They said they had already decided to send me to an Installment Loan School in Chicago. That did not appeal to me because I wanted to get out of consumer lending and become a commercial loan officer.

Chapter Three - 1965-1979

DIXIE COUNTY STATE BANK, CROSS CITY, FL

In January 1965, my brother, Lonnie, called to tell me about a bank job he heard about in Cross City, Florida. He gave me the President's name and phone number and I immediately called him. We agreed that we would meet in his office later that week. The next day I drove to Lonnie's home in Tallahassee and the next morning on to Cross City, 100 miles south of Tallahassee.

The President and Chairman of the Dixie County State Bank and I talked that afternoon. He showed me the bank's balance sheet and I told him I thought I could improve the bank's earnings. Little did he know that I had no idea how to do that and that looking at the balance sheet meant very little to me at that time. I was just "faking it until I could make it" but he did not seem to realize it. He offered me the job that afternoon. The beginning salary was $8,000 per year. He also agreed for the bank to pay all of my expenses and give me time off to attend the Banking School of the South at Louisiana State University (LSU). My first day working for Dixie County State Bank was March 15, 1965

The McKinney family-owned Dixie County State Bank. The current President's father had bought the bank in the 1950's and when he died, his son took over management of it. The Board of Directors consisted of the President-Chairman, his wife, his mother, his two brothers and another man whose father had been an officer of the bank before he died. The current President and Chairman had graduated from the Banking School at Louisiana State University (LSU) and therefore he recognized what a great school it was.

When I accepted, the job we sold our new home in Newnan and moved to Cross City, where we lived for the next fourteen years. There we bought a new two-bedroom concrete blockhouse on a dirt street across from the public housing complex. It was the only decent house available even though it only had two bedrooms and one bath. We paid $9,000 for it. Several years later, we built a two-story river house on the Suwannee River. It had three bedrooms, three baths, and a covered carport for our boat and my pickup truck.

I graduated from the LSU School in 1968. At that time, its name was School of Banking of the South. In 1985, I received a letter saying the school had decided that it was and had always been, a graduate-level school and therefore they had changed its name to the Graduate School of Banking of the South at LSU. The letter also said that if I would send them $25 they would send me a new certificate saying I had completed The Graduate School of Banking of the South at Louisiana State University. I now have two diplomas.

10 *This picture, taken at my Cross City office in 1968, shows my LSU class ring.*

That summer, in 1968, I attended fourteen weekly classes offered by a Dale Carnegie Professional Trainer. It was there that I received more training in public speaking, learned how to deal with various types of individuals and the ten ways to win friends and influence people. To this day, I can still recite those ten "ways". Recently, I wrote an article about them for a Central Florida Business Magazine. One of the best books that I received during those studies, was "How to Stop Worrying and Start Living". The Holy Bible is probably the only book, that taught me more about how to live without worry, than this book. Dale Carnegie first published it in 1948, but it is as relevant today as it was then. It is still available from Amazon.

When I accepted the job in Cross City, the President told me that my salary would increase as the bank prospered. In a few years, I noticed that the bank's income was increasing much faster than my salary. When I mentioned that to the President, he said he could not just keep giving me raises but he would come up with a bonus plan formula.

A few weeks later, he told me about the plan he had developed. He said, "The bank wanted a 1% return on assets and a 10% return on equity. Therefore, each year he would calculate the average of these two ratios expressed in dollars and I would receive one-half of 9% of the excess over the average of the ROA and ROE figures. The other one-half of the 9% would be held over to the next year at which time it would be added to the calculated figure for that year and I would receive one half of that total." I asked him how he came up with that formula. He said he wanted me to receive a $1,000 bonus the first year and that was what the formula calculated.

Little did I know how well that would turn out for me. The last year I worked there my bonus equaled 150% of my annual salary. This was the result of the "upside-down pyramid" structure of the bonus plan and because the bank became the highest performing bank in Florida that year. That achievement was published in a Miami Herald newspaper article on July 23, 1978.

In 1966, they promoted me to Vice President of the Bank and in 1967, when I was twenty-five, they elected me to their Board of Directors. They had been paying a Director's fee of $100 per month, but when they added me to the Board, they cut that to $75 so that the total director fee expense of the bank would not go up just because they had increased the number on the board by one.

Each year, at the Director's Organizational Meeting, they would ask me to leave the room while they voted on my salary. That usually took about five minutes. However, in January 1971, I was out of the room for about twenty minutes. When they finally called me back in they said, "Congratulations, we have elected you our new President." Frankly, I had never thought about ever being a Bank President and that position had never been discussed with me nor promised me. However, I gratefully accepted the position and my salary was increased to $14,400 per year. That was $1,200 per month or $6.92 per hour. I was 29 years old when I received this promotion.

Later I learned that it took the board twenty minutes to promote me because the Mother of the current President was objecting. It was her deceased husband, who had bought the bank originally and she did not like the idea of a non-family member being President of it. Her son, the current President, convinced her to change her mind by explaining that he would remain the Chairman of the Board and his office would still be in the bank building. He owned several other businesses and investments, which he managed from his bank office.

When we moved to Cross City, I did not realize how small the town was or how sparsely populated the county was. It was fifty miles to almost anywhere. Fifty miles to Perry, FL and fifty miles to Gainesville, FL. The town had a population of 1,700 and the county 5,000. There were no medical doctors, dentist or even veterinarians in the county, and it was fifty miles to the nearest hospital. The one funeral home did have a station wagon, which they used as an ambulance, and a hearse. One to take you to the hospital and the other to take you to the cemetery.

The town was about fifteen miles from Horseshoe Beach so, we thought, at least we could enjoy the beach. What we did not know was that Horseshoe Beach was a little fishing village and that there was not a sandy beach within 100 miles of it. The north county line was the Steinhatchee River and the south county line was the Suwannee River.

A timber company owned most of the land in the county. They leased large portions of it to ranchers for $0.25 per acre per year to graze their range cattle. Annually the ranchers would have a "round up" of the cattle they owned so they could brand them to show which rancher owned which cows. The leased land was not fenced off into designated pastures.

In addition, the timber company sold "hog claims" which allowed the holder of the claim to earmark hogs in that area indicating who had the right to them. The earmarks were cuttings made with a knife. Those particular markings were registered with the state.

To make loans on these range cows, we had to estimate the size of the herd. The county agent (agriculture expert hired by the University of Florida to advise farmers) would make an educated guess after examining the amount of cow manure in the area.

I tried to confirm his estimate by flying over the range in my airplane, a Cessna 172. I would tilt the wings, take pictures and later count the cattle shown in the photographs. I always wondered how I would round up, corral and transport the cows to market if I had to repossess them. Fortunately, that never happened.

Once I had to repossess a tractor-trailer rig. The owner gave me the keys and apologized because he had not been able to make the payments. I got up in the truck to drive it back to the bank before I realized that I had no idea how to start or drive such a vehicle. The customer was kind enough to drive it for me and I then took him home. He later was able to bring the payments current and I was glad to give him back the keys.

One Sunday afternoon, one of the Bank's Directors called me to say his son-in-law had flown a small plane to Cross City for a visit. He asked if I wanted to go for a ride in it. I said, "Of course." It would be the first time I had flown in a small plane. I was fascinated. The next week I told several friends about it. They too got interested in learning to fly so we agreed to go in together and buy a plane. I located one for sale in Tampa. That next Sunday a salesperson flew it to Cross City for us to preview. We all liked it and bought it on the spot.

In order to purchase the aircraft, I formed a small corporation, Cross City Aeronautics Inc. We each bought stock in the company and we each rented flying time by the hour from the corporation. This rental income made the monthly payments and covered the cost of insurance, fuel, maintenance, and repairs. Over the years, as I could and as others lost interest, I bought their stock. I owned it for ten years, flying it all over the southeast. The tail number was, 7759T. A local flight instructor helped each of us learn how to fly and get our pilot's license.

It would be easy to claim that becoming a pilot saved my life. Initially, to get a pilot's license, one has to pass a written test, a flying test, and a medical exam. The flying test (check ride) and a current medical certificate had to be updated every two years. While getting my annual physical in 1978 the Doctor said, "I can give you your medical certificate so you can continue to fly or, I can give you medicine to get your blood pressure down. However, you cannot have a valid pilot's license while taking these drugs." He said, "You are 37 years old and your blood pressure is 150/100. That is too high and it could make you have a heart attack." I said "You keep the certificate; I will take your medicine and sell the airplane."

My father and my brother both had already had heart attacks and I had been told twice that I had hypertension. Once was when I was being drafted into the Army. The Army decided I was not fit to fight because of my hypertension. When I told the Bank President that I was being drafted, he said that if I had to go into the Army, he would save my job for me and the bank would pay me the difference in my Army pay and my bank salary while I was gone.

This reminds me of the letter my college sent the selective service draft board in 1963. They were checking my status as a college student to determine if my student deferment should remain in force. The letter that Georgia State College sent the draft board was embarrassing but true. It read, "Mr. Roberts is enrolled at the college and his grades are in the upper half of the lower third of his class." In other words, I was on scholastic probation. That was because I never took the time to study. I was working a full-time job at the bank, had two-part-time jobs and I was attending school three nights a week at Georgia State College in Atlanta as well as attending the Georgia School of Banking at the University of Georgia in Athens in the summers. It was obvious that I was not letting my academic education interfere with my career and making a good income

I did attend college for four years, three at night as a part-time student, but did not accumulate enough credits to graduate. The four banking schools I attended, three at the graduate level, were all very helpful to my career. In addition, I have always taken advantage of attending seminars, conferences, and conventions and in recent years, webinars. However, I have learned a lot more by talking to other bankers, listening to bank examiners and staying current by reading industry periodicals.

Fortunately, no prospective employer has ever asked me if I had a degree. In retrospect, the only courses I took in college that helped my career was accounting and perhaps business writing. I really enjoyed learning accounting but it did not come easy to me. I failed Accounting 101 and Accounting 102 but passed both of them on the second try.

I was fortunate that the Newnan bank had paid all my expenses to attend college for three years plus the cost of me attending and graduating from the three-year Georgia School of Banking at the University of Georgia. All total, I attended thirteen years of higher education at six colleges or universities. My employers paid the cost of all of these schools except for my first year at West Georgia College.

Two things I learned from bankers, not while I was in the classroom, but while attending LSU, was how to make money on the side and how to reduce my living expenses. The first, how to make money on the side, could be accomplished by starting an insurance agency and offering to insure the automobiles the bank financed. The second was to have the bank furnish me a car for my personal use at the bank's expense. I proposed these ideas to the bank's president when I graduated and he approved them both. What started out small, as a side business, grew over the years and there were times that I was making more money selling insurance than I was being paid by the bank.

The bank president justified his decision to furnish me a bank car by deciding to sell the $6,000 Oldsmobile the bank was furnishing him and have the bank buy two $3,000 cars. One for him and one for me. My first bank car was a new 1968 Ford. Future bank employers furnished me cars for the next forty years. Later, instead of a bank car, I received a liberal automobile allowance . . . usually $1,000 per month.

The Dixie County State Bank had less than four million dollars in assets when I joined their staff. It was the only bank in the county and its nearest competitor was twenty-five miles south on US Highway 19. The Dixie County Bank, in 1965, operated very similar to the way it had been operating since its organization in 1923. Daily entries, made in a leather-bound book with pen and ink, were then posted on a mechanical posting machine to ledger sheets. Totals from the general ledger sheets were printed daily on a one-page balance sheet using a wide- carriage-adding machine.

Bond Accounting was one of my duties. That involved using ink pens to record in a large leather-covered book all securities bought or sold, the interest income received, as well as calculating and posting the accretion of securities purchased at a discount or the amortization of any bought at a premium.

I did similar record-keeping for all of the Bank's fixed assets. This included calculating and posting the depreciation on each item using the double-declining balance method or the straight-line method, whichever produced the largest expense for tax purposes.

Checks and deposits were posted twice on the same mechanical posting machines as the general ledger. Once on a ledger sheet which the bank kept as its permanent record and then on a statement that was mailed to the customer. There were no teller machines, no "cash in" or "cash-out" tickets, no proof machines and no debit or credit tickets and of course no computers.

I did not realize, until I got to the bank, that their accounting was on the "cash basis" not the "accrual basis." A few years later, we did convert to the accrual method. Initially, this brought many major changes to the income statement and the capital accounts. Cash-based accounting records income and expenses when received and paid. Accrual based accounting records income and expenses as they are earned and incurred. The accrual bases is the only accounting method used by banks now. It is much more accurate.

It was surprising to me to learn that the President of the Dixie County Bank did not know anything about debits and credits. To help him learn and understand basic accounting, I made notes for him on the top of a daily statement that read, "Debit accounts on the left, credit accounts on the right. To increase a debit account, debit it. To decrease a debit account, credit it. To Increase a credit account, credit it and to decrease a credit account debit it. That daily statement, with those notes on it, was still tacked on his wall, above his desk, when I left the bank, fourteen years later.

By the time I left Cross City, December 1978, the bank had been completely automated with all accounting and processing being performed on computers in Tallahassee. The bank was modernized and it had become the **highest performing bank** in Florida with a return on equity of 20.8% and a return on assets of 2.25%. The yield on average earning assets was 10.12%, the cost of funds, 3.25% resulting in a net interest spread of 6.87%. This means the bank's profits as measured by the bank's equity divided by its net income was the best of all banks in the state when compared by percentages. This was the result of the bank's "spread", interest income minus interest expense, being better than most all other banks in the state when compared by percentages. Other factors included maximizing non-interest income and minimizing non-interest expenses. We compared favorably in all of these categories.

The high yields on earning assets were attributable to the interest we earned financing automobiles and mobile homes. Interest rates on those loans were calculated using either the add-on or the discount methods resulting in yields nearly double the stated rate. Of course, this was before banks had to disclose the annual percentage rate, APR, and simple interest rate calculations were not used on installment (consumer) loans. Most every loan also included credit life insurance on which the bank made a large profit. The cost for this insurance was 1% and the bank would receive about one half of that as a commission.

As the bank became known as an aggressive, high performing community bank, I started getting invitations to speak to various groups. The first of these speeches was to a joint meeting of the Florida Bankers Association and the Florida Forestry Association where I spoke on Financing Logging Equipment. I also spoke at an annual Florida Bankers Association and a Florida Independent Bankers annual convention on High-Performance Banking. This led to an invitation for me to be a panel member at the Bank Administration Institute (BAI) Bank President's Forum in Scottsdale, Arizona. All of these presentations were in the 1970s.

11 This picture of me was taken when I spoke at a joint meeting of the Florida Bankers Association and the Florida Forestry Association in 1970.

Before 1977, Branch banking offices were not legal in Florida. Every bank building was a separate bank with its own charter, Board of Directors and executive offices. Every bank had to have a President and a Cashier. The Presidents usually did the lending or had loan officers who did and reported to him. The Cashier usually handled operations. What was then a Cashier position is now the Chief Financial or Chief Operations Officer.

Branch Banking did not become legal in Florida until 1977. After branching became legal, instead of starting a new bank to expand its market area, a bank could get permission to build a branch office. However, originally, a bank could not branch across county lines. Later a new law allowed banks to have branches anywhere in the state and eventually they could branch nationwide.

Before branch banking became legal, bank holding companies became prevalent. They were a special type of corporation, supervised by the Federal Reserve. Bank Holding Companies could own several banks. However, they could not own other type businesses.

In 1978, the Dixie County State Bank opened one of the first Branch Banks in the state. It was a doublewide mobile building, which we bought from the Ellis Banking Company in Port Richey, Fl. and then moved to Steinhatchee, FL. The cost of the building was $25,000. That included all its equipment and furnishings except the safe deposit boxes. Those cost an additional $10,000. When I heard the mobile banking unit was available, my seven-year-old son, Wes, and I flew my 1960 Cessna 172 to see the unit and try to buy it. When the banker told me he would sell it for $25,000, I asked him if he would take a personal check. He agreed. I was concerned he might realize the unit was worth much more and he would sell it to someone else if I did not close the deal on the spot.

By the beginning of the twenty-first century, bank consolidation and banks closed by bank regulators began shrinking the total number of banks across the country and in Florida. When I moved to Florida in 1965 there were 750 banks in the state, in 2004, when I was President of the Florida Bankers Association, there were 325 in the state. In 2020, there are only about 100. Across the nation, the number has dropped from over 18,000 to less than 5,000.

As soon as we moved to Cross City, I became very involved in the community. My wife and I attended the First Baptist Church where we both sang in the choir, I joined the local Rotary Club and later became its President and I also became involved in the Chamber of Commerce and later became President. I received appointments from two Governors to serve on the Northwest Florida Housing Authority and the Suwannee River Authority. The River Authority had one person from each county that bordered the river serving on its board. I also served on the Lake City Community College Foundation Board.

Within a year or two, I became interested in being on the City Council. However, I lost my first bid for the seat. The person who defeated me could neither read nor write but he could get more votes. Two years later, I ran for Mayor and Municipal Judge. In my first run for a seat on the City Council, I thought I knew how to organize a campaign because I had taken a Political Science course at West Georgia College. As it turned out, that course did not teach politics the way they were practiced in Cross City, FL.

I prepared better for my second political race by visiting the County Sheriff. He was the master politician in the county. I told him that I was running for Mayor and that I knew I would need his help. He said, "I will help you, but not because I like you . . . in fact, I don't". He went on to explain that one of my opponents, a local second-generation grocery store owner, had not supported him in his last election, so he would help me to get back at him.

The Sheriff then said, "You have two opponents. One, an older man, who will go door to door asking for votes, saying he needs the $50 per month Mayor's fee. He will get the sympathy vote. The grocer is a redneck; he will get the long hair, wide belt buckle votes. You will get the silk-stocking vote. That leaves the black people and I will get you their votes." He did and I won. I was 28 years old.

As it turned out the Mayor had very little to do with running the city which is what I wanted to do. He could veto actions of the City Council; however, I never had a need to do that. Annually, I did make "State of the City" addresses to any organization interested in hearing how the city was doing.

12 Here is a picture of me when I was the Mayor of Cross City, Florida in 1968. I was presenting the keys to a new police car to the town's police chief, "Punk" Clark.

The Mayor was also the Municipal Judge. I knew very little about how to be a Judge except what I had learned from a compassionate county judge in the neighboring county six years early. I tried to conduct my court sessions in a similar manner. However, that nearly backfired on me.

One man from a neighboring county appeared in my court to plead not guilty to a traffic ticket he had received from our Police Chief. I found him guilty but suspended his fine because he had driven 100 miles to appear and I thought that was punishment enough. The City Council threatened to impeach me for returning the man's bond and not making him pay a fine. I told the City Council members that was ok with me and while we were at it, I would bring impeachment charges against several of them for approving city workers, using city equipment, to do work on private property. That was illegal. They decided to drop the subject.

Another case involved the son of a local prominent resident. The boy had received a traffic ticket for reckless driving and speeding. I knew that having him pay a fine would not be a determent to him repeating the offense. Therefore, I sentenced him to work on the city garbage truck every afternoon after school for a week. He told me he would not do that so I told the Chief of Police to lock him up. The accused then changed his mind, worked on the garbage truck, and never came back to my court.

After serving as Mayor for two years, I once again ran for a city council seat. That time I won and two years later, re-elected. Three of those four years, I served as President of the City Council.

During my tenure with the city, we built a new City Hall building and a new fire station. We also bought the first new fire truck the city had ever had to replace the WWII surplus fire truck the city had been using. We also paved all the dirt streets in the town and enticed a company to bring cable TV to our town. The last time I ran a political campaign for a city council seat I pledged, that if re-elected, I would have the city pave the street in front of my house and build two new tennis courts for the public to use. As you might suspect, I had recently started playing tennis. I was re-elected and those projects were completed.

While studying how to be a judge, I learned that Florida had passed a standardized traffic ticket law. It was apparent to me that our one-man police department was not using them. The Police Chief used some preprinted forms, which he required anyone he stopped to fill out with their name, address and driver's license number. He would then stamp his name on the bottom of the form. All of this was necessary because he could not read or write.

To address this, I asked the Chief to stop by my home one evening. While sitting in my living room, I told him that I realized that he had not been able to get an education and therefore had problems reading driver's licenses and filling out forms. He angrily told me he could read. I asked him to read me the information on my license. When he could not, I offered to have him come to my home as often as necessary for me to teach him how to read and write. He refused, stood up, took off his badge and gun and said, "Let's just step outside and settle this."

That did not happen, but it did make him mad enough to resign the job he had held for nearly twenty years. The city then hired its first experienced, certified Police Chief who could read and write.

In 1978, I ran for a seat on the Board of Education. To politic for that position, I bought an old pickup truck. Most males in the county drove pickup trucks with a long whip antenna for their CB radio, a dog box in the back of the truck and a gun rack on the window. None of that helped me win the race. I lost to a woman. That meant that I had lost one race to a man who could not read or write and another to a woman. It was then that I gave up politics and decided it was better to know one (a politician) than to be one.

While living in Dixie Count we were blessed with the birth of a son. We named him Weston Lamar Roberts. He was born January 19, 1968, in the Alachua Hospital in Gainesville, which, as I mentioned earlier, was fifty miles from our home.

Wes, as we called him, was named after his maternal grandfather, Weston Tidwell. We doted on him in every way possible, taking him everywhere we could and trying to give him anything he wanted. He received a rifle before he was old enough to have one and a train track set up. The trains were really for me since I did not have one as a child. He also wore out two go-cart. We enjoyed taking him down the Suwannee River in our boat and watching him water ski past the alligators. He was always a good student and most usually well behaved.

There was a time that he misbehaved in Church. When we got home, I addressed his behavior by saying, "If you were a father, and you had a son who misbehaved as you did today, what would you do?" He thought for a moment and then said very seriously, "I would tell that young man that if he ever did that again, I would tear his butt up." I had trouble not laughing. He did not get a spanking.

His mother and I did travel some. When Wes could not go with us, his Grandmother Roberts, my mother, would come from Georgia, where she lived, to stay with him and his dog, "Ginny," a beautiful Dalmatian.

Our trips included a Caribbean Cruise, trips to California, Hawaii and 3 trips to Europe to attend International Banking Seminars. Those trips, sponsored by a correspondent bank, were paid for by my bank. We traveled to England, France, Germany, Belgium, and Switzerland to attend the seminars.

There was a time in the mid-'70s when I told my medical doctor that I was depressed or despondent. He sent me to a Psychologist who had me tell him my life story. The Doctor quickly analyzed my condition and told me that I needed more challenges and goals.

He went on to explain that at age 35, I had accomplished more than most men had by age 65. He recounted the facts that I had given him. He said, "You have completed ten years of higher education, been elected Mayor, Municipal Judge, President of the City Council, President of the Rotary Club, and President of the Chamber of Commerce. You became a Bank President at age 29, own an insurance agency, been President of a manufacturing company, been a church and community leader, own two homes, a boat and an airplane, and traveled across the country including Hawaii and Europe." He repeated, "You need new goals and challenges." The ones you had, have been achieved. That made sense to me and I started planning accordingly. I did not need any pills or additional counseling.

Chapter Four – 1979-1981

FLORIDA NATIONAL BANK OF BREVARD

When I left the Cross City bank in December 1978, Joyce moved back to Georgia with Wes while I was settling into my new job. In February 1979, I became the President and CEO of the Florida National Bank of Brevard County. My office was in Titusville and we built a new branch office in Melbourne. My annual salary was $30,000.

13 *A newspaper ad that announced me joining the Bank*

Joyce and Wes never rejoined me. She filed for divorce and later, on September 25, 1982, she died at age 39. Wes, then fourteen years of age, came to live with me.

The Florida National Bank Holding Company owned the Florida National Bank of Brevard and about twenty-seven other banks. Those were located from Key West to Pensacola. Their headquarters was in Jacksonville. A member of the DuPont family originally owned these banks as well as many other businesses. When the patriot of that family died, his brother-in-law, Ed Ball, became the trustee of the estate. Mr. Ball managed the bank holding company, the Southeast Railroad and the St. Joe Paper Company, all of which had been owned by Mr. DuPont.

Three major events occurred in my life while working for Florida National Bank.

I remarried, I completed the National Graduate Commercial Lending School at the University of Oklahoma, and I was promoted to the Bank's Holding Company Headquarters in Jacksonville.

Debbie Gooding and I married in Melbourne, FL, August 23, 1979. We honeymooned on St John's Island in the Caribbean and bought a home in Indian Harbour Beach, near Melbourne, FL. She worked for a Savings and Loan Association there. Debbie was young, cute and smart. We enjoyed playing tennis, water skiing, horseback riding, and snow skiing together.

While living in Brevard County, I attended The National Graduate Commercial Lending School at the University of Oklahoma. It was a two-year program. During that time, I completed case studies and wrote papers. It was the best of the four banking schools I attended. My studies included commercial lending, analyzing financial statements, underwriting complex credits, performing loan reviews as well as asset-liability management. In fact, I enjoyed it so much that I returned to Norman, Oklahoma several years later to visit with my favorite professor. He had written a book on Asset Liability Management for the American Bankers Association.

As I was completing this graduate school, the students were given the opportunity to take an additional test. Those who passed it earned the professional designation, Certified Commercial Lender (CCL). I passed. Later I heard about another Professional Designation, Certified Lender-Business Banking (CLBB). While applying for it, I learned that my experience and education were all the qualifications I needed. Therefore, they grandfathered me into the program and gave me that additional professional designation.

While visiting with the President of the Bank Holding Company in Jacksonville, I mentioned the three banking schools I had completed and the two professional designations I had. He said that the regulators (bank examiners) had recently told him and their Board of Directors that the holding company needed a Loan Review Department. The Holding Company, which at that time had two billion dollars in assets, owned twenty-seven banks in Florida. Because of my qualifications and the fact that I had been making loans for twenty years, he promoted me to Vice President of the Holding Company in charge of Loan Review for all their banks in the state.

It was an honor to be promoted to that position, but it was not what I wanted to do. I had been a community bank president for about ten years at that time and I really enjoyed that position. However, he persisted, and I started traveling the state digging through loan files and writing up my banker friends for not documenting or underwriting their loans according to the bank's policies or the regulator's requirements.

Chapter Five – 1981-1991

FIRST NATIONAL BANK, FORT WALTON BEACH, FL

While on one of those trips to the Florida panhandle I visited with my friend, Jimmy Tringas, who owned controlling interest and was the Board Chairman of the First National Bank in Fort Walton Beach. Jimmy and I had become friends while attending International Banking Seminars in Europe. He had just fired his President because the bank was not growing nor making money, and he was looking for a replacement.

I suggested that he promote his son, John, the bank's Executive Vice President, to fill the President's position. He said that John had declined the offer. Jimmy offered the job to me and I accepted. My starting date was February 1, 1981, and my beginning salary was $40,000 per year. One of my benefits was to be a new car.

14 This picture of me was taken in 1981 when I became President of the First National Bank in Fort Walton Beach, FL

However, once I got there, I learned that the $72 million asset bank could not afford a new car. That meant that I had to drive an old Buick that had been provided the former president. Within a couple of years, the bank's income and growth had improved and the bank could provide me the new car they had promised.

Mr. Tringas asked what type of car I wanted. I reminded him that we had agreed on a new Oldsmobile. He said they did not buy Oldsmobile's because the dealer did not bank with First National. He then surprised me by offering me a new Cadillac. I was very pleased with that offer; however, he stipulated that it had to be the lowest priced model. I politely said I had never driven the lowest priced model of any car and that I would be glad to pay the difference if I could upgrade to the top model. He then graciously agreed for me to buy the Cadillac of my choosing, a big Fleetwood.

As we were moving to northwest Florida, Debbie said she would need something to do. She said, "I need a job, a horse or a baby." I said, "For gosh sakes, go buy a horse." She did, then she surprised me a month later by telling me we were expecting a child. Not long after the baby was born, she got the job she wanted which was selling real estate. So, all three of her wishes had then been fulfilled.

She bought a registered Thorough Bred horse trained for Western or English riding. The name on its registration papers was "Grand Finale" but we called him "Grandy". When Debbie could no longer ride him, because of the pregnancy, I took riding lessons. It was not long before I could trot, gallop, run and jump rails. I even jumped him bareback one time. Of course, that was the result of a dare. After our baby was born, Debbie rode Grandy, showed him frequently and won several blue ribbons.

15 One of my favorite pictures, taken in 1983, of Grandy with Jay, our son, sitting with me on the saddle. He was about eighteen months old at that time.

For years, I enjoyed riding horses almost anywhere we went. Below are pictures of two of those events.

16 Lamar making a Palomino rear up In Puerto Rico.

17 Lamar, on a quarter horse, barrel racing at a Dude Ranch in Colorado, 1989

Our son, Jay, was born on November 8, 1981. We named him Jay Lamar Roberts. He was a delightful addition to our family. We picked the name Jay after the first bank President I worked for, Jay Smith. Of course, his middle name is my middle name, and the same middle name of his older brother, Weston Lamar Roberts. I wanted both of the boys to be named Lamar but I did not want either to be a "Jr". His first name "Jay" also gave him the same initials as mine, JLR, and made his name similar to mine since I usually sign, J. Lamar Roberts.

The next September, I received a telephone call from my mother saying that my first wife, Joyce had died. Wes, my oldest son, who was then fourteen, came to live with Debbie, Jay and me. He was a welcomed addition. I now had both boys living with me. The brothers always got along well even though there was a fourteen-year age difference.

Wes made many friends easily; played football in Junior High and did well in High School. He usually had a part-time job. His first car was not one of his choosing. I selected it for him, a four-door sedan, which the bank had recently repossessed and I bought. He quickly traded it for an MG Midget. It did not give him good service so he bought a used Honda and later a 280 ZX.

He liked the "Z" cars so much that over the next ten years or so, he bought two more, owning all three at the same time. They were his passion until he bought a new anniversary edition Corvette. He still owns that car in addition to a couple of Mercedes and a Denali. Wes has also owned several bikes, a crotch rocket motorcycle and now a large Harley Davidson Motorcycle that his wife bought for him.

He graduated from Choctaw High School in Fort Walton Beach, FL then Tallahassee Community College and eventually Florida State University in Tallahassee. His degree from FSU is in Management Information Systems. General Electric recruited him at an above-average starting salary as he was graduating from FSU. That was because, in his last several years at FSU, he had worked for the University in the field of his degree. Therefore, he had not only the education but also the experience GE needed. He is now a Computer Sales Engineer for Palo Alto Networks, a nationwide company that manufactures and sells cybersecurity solutions.

Jay also did well in school, playing football (I was thrilled to see him make a touch down one night) for and graduating from Fort Walton High in Fort Walton Beach. He went on to graduate from Santa Fe Community College, then from the University of Florida in Gainesville with a degree in History and later from Florida Coastal School of Law in Jacksonville. He is now a Shareholder with a large Florida law firm, Becker, and is one of the few Attorneys in Florida certified in Condominium and Planned Development Law.

At an early age, Kathy, the woman who helped raise him, cared for Jay, His Mother got her Real Estate Agent license believing that was a career that she wanted to pursue. She was not very successful selling real estate but this led her to become an excellent and successful Real Estate Appraiser. Now, thirty years later, she has owned her firm for many years and is well known and respected for the services she provides.

Within a couple of years, the First National Bank of Fort Walton Beach returned to profitability and started to grow. It grew $100,000,000 during my tenure there. Because of its success, the family that owned control of it decided they wanted to buy out the minority shareholders in order to own 100% of the bank. To accomplish this, we sought expert legal advice, formed a one-bank holding company and proceeded to do a reverse triangle merger. This would result in the minority shareholders being required to sell their shares at a fair market price to the majority shareholders. It was a legal maneuver.

One shareholder took exception to "having" to sell his shares. He convinced other minority shareholders to join him in a class-action lawsuit against the Bank's Board of Directors and Executive Officers. Therefore, each of us was individually, sued for $25,000,000. We did settle the case and accomplish what we set out to do but at an extra cost of about $500,000. I thought that was a big compliment for anyone to think I had or could get $25,000,000. As it turned out the bank did not have any insurance to pay for the defense.

We also planned to build a ten-story building to house the bank, the executive offices, and some rental space. I believe the cost was to be about ten million dollars. The financing was approved but we were not able to lease the excess space and therefore the building could not be built. Unfortunately, we had signed a contract with the builder and that cost another $500,000 to get out of it.

We also messed up getting too aggressive financing speculative ventures with contractors building investment condominiums in the beach areas. When President Reagan's tax revision in the mid-1980 reduced the tax incentive for investors to buy these type units, many of our loans became 'workouts'. Of course, the regulators took us to task for making the loans. Not when we went into the projects but when they did not sell and payoff as planned. They have such excellent hindsight. I do not recall what this cost the bank but I do remember that it was an expensive venture and an education on what type of loans we should not make.

One unusual loan the bank made was to finance the property for the new *Bob Hope Village for Air Force Enlisted Widows*. The one-million-dollar loan was unusual because it was to a new nonprofit organization that had no collateral to pledge and no one to guarantee payment. However, Fort Walton Beach was an Air Force town and we felt sure the village was needed and would be successful. It also had the support of Bob Hope, one of the biggest names in show business at the time. Mr. Hope committed to coming to the area every other year for several years to put on a fundraiser for the Village. The Village originally had 64 units. It now has 445 units. The loan was paid in full, on time.

18 This picture was taken as I greeted Bob Hope and Miss USA, October 1989 when they arrived at the Destin Airport in Mr. Hope's private jet. They were in town to raise money for the Bob Hope Village. I greeted them as President of the Fort Walton Chamber of Commerce.

To better train our employees, we started our own, First National Bank School of Banking. It was set up with assistance from the local Community College. The school had three levels. The first was for all new employees. It taught them the rudiments of banking including the bank's policies and procedures. The second level was for those employees who were supervisors or who wanted to advance to supervisory positions. It included subjects on how to manage employees, maintain or improve morale, deal with non-performers as well as requirements and restrictions dictated by human resource laws. The third level was for officers and department heads. It mainly included employees attending banking schools, seminars and conferences offered by the banking industry. During that time, I completed the Graduate School of Bank Investments at the University of Oklahoma.

My involvement in the banking industry led to many speaking engagements for me. They included the ABA/BMA Community Bankers Conference in California on "Incentive Pay," the Arkansas Association of Bank Holding Companies Convention in Little Rock, Arkansas on "Business Development," the Graduate School of Banking at the University of Wisconsin on "Developing a Sales Culture," and the Florida Bank Presidents' Summit on "What Keeps Bankers Awake at Night".

Later, I was on the Board of the Florida Bankers Association's (FBA) Florida School of Banking at the University of Florida. There I lectured on Bank Management and Leadership. My FBA involvement also included being the Director of their Branch Managers Institute, Chairman of the Board of the Florida Bankers Insurance Trust and Chairman of the FBA's Education Council.

As in other towns where I worked as a banker, I was very involved in the community. This included becoming President of the Fort Walton Beach Chamber of Commerce and President of the Okaloosa County Committee of 100, which was later renamed the Economic Development Committee.

One of the major accomplishments of the Chamber of Commerce during my year as President was the passage of the "Bed Tax," more accurately called the Tourist Development Tax. The effort to get this tax approved by the voters had been defeated twice in previous years. There were those who were opposed to the tax because they knew the money would be used to advertise the area and attract more tourists. They did not want any more tourists coming to their local beaches. Others opposed it because they thought the county was actually going to make them pay a tax for each bed they owned. Actually, the tax is on hotel room rentals and is similar to a sales tax. Over the years, the total collection has increased. For example, in 1993-94, the total collected was $1,683,000 and in 2017-18, the total collected had increased to $19,653,000. That money, used to promote tourism in the Destin, Fort Walton Beach area, has been very effective.

I was also an organizing director of the Okaloosa Walton Community College Foundation and served as its first Treasurer. The Foundation now has assets exceeding $51,000,000. It is satisfying for me to see how these initiatives, which started small, have grown to be what they are today.

The local Chamber of Commerce had a Military Affairs Committee, MAC. Membership was very limited. Those privileged to be a member were involved with the three Air Force Bases in Okaloosa County. I was fortunate to be a member of this elite group. The bases in the county included Eglin Air Force Base, Hurlbert Field, and Duke Field. The MAC members attended the military's social and special events and the Military brass attended ours. In addition, we frequently traveled to other Air Forces Bases across the country as their guests.

Annually, a few MAC members were named "Honorary Commanders" of various units on the base. It was my privilege to be the Honorary Commander of the 20th SOS. This unit flew large helicopters out of Hurlbert Field training the airmen to conduct low-level penetration in hostile enemy territory, to accomplish clandestine infiltration and exfiltration, aerial gunnery support and resupply special operations forces throughout the world. Some of my rides with them included me shooting a mounted machine gun out a side door and being on board when the helicopter was being refueled while airborne.

Being a member of MAC also provided me the opportunity to fly on other type airplanes. These experiences included flying left seat for one hour in an Air Force C130 while cannons were being shot out of it and flying in an F15 while it participated in a midair electronic gunfight with another F15 that was on the same training mission. I also had the experience of landing on the aircraft carrier, Lexington, while it was in the Gulf of Mexico. That flight was in a Navy, Carrier on Board (COB), a high wing twin-engine plane. We spent the day on the Lexington and that evening, were catapulted off, to fly back to the airport in Pensacola.

19 This picture was taken of me in 1988 at Eglin Air Force Base, Fort Walton Beach, Florida when I was boarding an F15 jet fighter plane for the ride of my life. Notice the two names on the fuselage just below the windshield.

Riding in the F15 was the only time I have ever worn a parachute or a "g" suit. The "g" suit was like an additional pair of pants that went over my flight pants. It was connected to the plane by a suction hose, which made the suit squeeze my legs when the plane was pulling negative "g's". This squeezing action forced blood back to my head, to keep me from passing out.

During the 1980s, there was a lot of talk in Congress about closing military bases. Several bases were closed because they were thought not to be needed and that closing them would reduce expenses, thereby saving tax dollars. It was a major concern for the Fort Walton Beach area since the three bases in the county contributed greatly to the local economy.

In an effort to minimize the economic impact closures in our area might have, three MAC members went to Washington DC, to meet with various Air Force Generals. I was one of three who were honored to go with Congressman, Earl Hutto, to the Pentagon. I do not know if what we said or did had anything to do with the results but I do know that none of our bases were shut down or reduced in size. In fact, we picked up another unit at Eglin that moved from a base that closed in California. It did not hurt that our Congressman served on the congressional committee that appropriated funds for military bases.

When we moved to Fort Walton Beach in 1981, it became apparent that the social club to join was "Billy Bowlegs". It had been in existence for thirty or forty years and resembled the Mardi Gras organizations in Mobile and New Orleans. It was a social club with only one purpose, having fun. Debbie and I joined and quickly were caught up in all the partying and fun activates they organized. Many events were formal, black tie, and others were pirate-themed. It was a big deal each year when the new "Billy" was announced as well as who he had selected as his Queen. Debbie was selected for this honor in the late '80s.

This type of socializing never appealed to me because I am not now, nor have I ever been a party person. While I am not opposed to anyone drinking in moderation or dancing, I have seen harm come to individuals and couples who did not enjoy this type of partying appropriately. Debbie enjoyed the atmosphere I did not. That contributed to our divorce. Another contributing factor was our age difference. I am eighteen years older than her.

In 1991, I moved to Merritt Island, Florida to work at the American Bank of the South. The President and Chairman offered me the position of President with him remaining the Bank's Chairman. I accepted but when I reported to work, he said he had changed his mind and could not give up the President's title. He said I could be the bank's Executive Vice President in charge of operations and retail. The bank had sixteen branches at that time.

When I accepted his original offer, I turned down the opportunity to be President of a smaller bank in Gainesville. Both banks offered the same annual salary, $80,000 per year. When I realized that I would not be President of the American Bank, I called the Chairman of the Gainesville bank to see if the President's position there was still available. Unfortunately, it was not.

Not only did the Chairman of the Merritt Island Bank mislead me about the position, he did not tell me that the bank was "a troubled institution and was being placed under a consent agreement by the regulators, That being a fact, it turned out that I was better off not becoming president of a bank that was in trouble. After working together for about one year he told me the bank did not need both of us. I agreed and left. A few years later the Chairman and President was removed by the regulators and the bank was required to merge with another bank to keep it from failing.

Chapter Six – Marrying Cindy

One of the best things that happened to me while living in Merritt Island was my marriage to Cindy Roberts, April 18, 1992. You will notice that her last name was already "Roberts" (no relation), so she did not even have to change her name on her driver's license, just her address. When she joined me in Merritt Island, she immediately wanted something to do. I suggested that since she had attended Auburn University for one year, she could finish her AA degree at the local Brevard County College. That only took a few months. She then commuted to the University of Central Florida in Orlando where she graduated with a Bachelor of Science Degree in Psychology.

Shortly after we moved to Pasco County, she enrolled at the University of South Florida in Tampa where she completed her Master's Degree in Gerontology with an "A" in every course. They must have known she would be an outstanding student because, before she attended her first class, the Dean of the School, called to see if she would like to be a teacher's assistant. That offer included a private office, a salary and the waiver of her tuition. A few years later, she completed her Doctoral Studies for a Doctor of Education degree in Psychology. Unfortunately, she did not have the opportunity to complete her thesis and so her official degree designation is MSABD, which represents **M**aster of **S**cience, **A**ll **B**ut **D**issertation. About fifteen years later, she completed a one-year postgraduate curriculum earning the designation, Certified Parenting Coach.

Cindy has been "the apple of my eye" for years. She is younger than I, beautiful, very smart, a philanthropist at heart (I like to see how much money I can make. She likes to see how much she can give to help others,) and her personality draws people to her. Strangers approach her, tell their life story, and ask her for advice while not even noticing that I am standing beside her. She also has three daughters who are very dear to me, Allison, Amy, and Alana. They are all grown now, have college degrees, husbands and children. With my two boys, mentioned earlier, we now proudly say we have five children plus one (explained later). We do not refer to the children as hers, or mine. They are simply ours and treated accordingly.

At one time, either one of our children or their spouse was a marketing executive, a teacher, a preacher, a doctor, a lawyer or an engineer. The marketing executive has quit marketing, the teacher has quit teaching and the preacher has quit preaching but all have good careers. We are blessed to have such a family!

The "plus one" I referred to earlier is our first Granddaughter, Kaylie Marie Caraway, born November 13, 1998. Her mother and father lived in Crestview Florida at that time. When Kaylie was eleven months old, she and her mother came to visit us. Kaylie never left. Cindy and I, mostly Cindy, have raised her. She is now twenty-one and just completed her senior year at the University of South Florida. Her plans are to get a Master's Degree and then attend Medical School. Previously she graduated from Lee Academy for Gifted Education in Tampa, which she attended for fourteen years.

Kaylie has traveled extensively with Cindy and me. She has now been to over half the states in the USA and more than twenty foreign countries. At Lee Academy, she had many years of Latin, French, and Spanish and she has had the opportunity to use this education during her travels.

"Sugar," my nickname for Cindy, is an excellent cook, great trip planner, homemaker, financial manager, my best friend and a great mother to our children and grandmother to our grandchildren. Our grandchildren call her "Nana"; they call me "Grandy". She has stuck by my side through thick and thin never asking for more than I could give and always supporting my various career and industry endeavors.

We enjoy our involvement in our church, our grandchildren and especially traveling. One of our big projects was planning, designing, furnishing, landscaping and decorating our dream home. It would mean little to others, but it is exactly what we wanted. We did have an award-winning architect design our house and the company that designed and built our pool won third place in the world for a pool he had designed.

Our travels have taken us throughout North American, including Alaska and Hawaii, Canada, Mexico, Puerto Rica, and the Caribbean. In addition, we have vacationed in many of the European countries, as far north as Norway and Russia and as far south as Greece and Israel. These trips have been by buses, trains, planes, riverboats and cruise ships.

New York and Paris are two of Cindy's favorites. Washington DC and Amsterdam are two of mine, but Israel was the one we both enjoyed the most and where we would like to visit again. A train took us across Canada; this was the least enjoyable of our travels. The cruises had us sailing the Pacific Ocean (around the Hawaiian Islands and Alaska), the Atlantic Ocean (around Great Britain), as well as the Mediterranean, Baltic and Adriatic Seas. The river cruises included the Rhine and the Danube and a flight in a small airplane took us just north of the Arctic Circle.

Our trip to France was a little out of the ordinary. We were there for Christmas and New Year's, 2013. While there, we celebrated Cindy's birthday, December 26th. Her request for this trip was so that, on her birthday, she could be "Sipping Dom Perignon in France". Therefore, on that day, a private guide took us to the Moet & Chandon Winery where we had a private underground tour of where the Dom Perignon Champaign is stored and aged. We also enjoyed a bottle of "Dom" in their private dining room with their Sommelier. Of course, on New Year's Eve, night, we celebrated with the Parisians on the Champs-Elysees.

20 This picture of the Eiffel Tower in Paris, France was a perfect place for a birthday kiss.

Cindy has also arranged several special events for me. Knowing how much I enjoy flying, she arranged for me to fly a single-seat para-plane (motorized parachute), and a glider (no engine). The glider did have an instructor on board. Neither required that I have a current pilot's license. Cindy and I also rode, as the only passengers, on a blimp to celebrate our anniversary. Jay, Wes and I enjoyed a hot air balloon ride while we were skiing in Colorado, in the '80s.

Chapter Seven – 1992-2009

FIRST NATIONAL BANK OF PASCO

I joined First National Bank of Pasco (FNBP) in Dade City, Florida as its President and CEO in June 1992. A correspondent banker, Greg Rains, knew I was looking for a new challenge so he arranged for me to meet the Chairman of the bank. The bank had advertised the position in the Wall Street Journal and had received over 360 resumes. While being interviewed by the Board of Directors, one of the Directors asked me if I could save the bank. I said, "I do not know if it can be saved but if it can, I think I can do it."

In 1986, First National Bank of Pasco organized with $3,180,000 in capital. When I joined them in June 1992, it had never made a profit; the capital had shrunk to about $1,500,000 and, it was continuing to lose money monthly. The Bank Examiners said the bank's capital was deficient, its asset quality unacceptable, its management incapable, its earnings insufficient to increase capital to a satisfactory level and its liquidity was below par.

Because of these conditions, the Office of the Comptroller of the Currency, OCC, (bank examiners) placed the bank under a Consent Agreement. In other words, the bank's management, executive officers and the Board of Directors, would have to abide by the agreement and improve the condition of the bank or the bank would be closed by the OCC. This also meant the bank had been designated a "troubled financial institution."

I had only been there four months when the regulators (OCC) from Atlanta and Tampa met with the bank's Board of Directors and me to say they had decided the bank could not be saved and therefore they would be closing it. The two previous bank presidents had been fired because of the bank's condition and their inability to correct the deficiencies. However, the examiners did not follow through with their plans to close the bank and I did not learn why for more than ten years.

In 2005 I had dinner at Joe's Crab House in South Miami Beach with the then Comptroller of the Currency, John Dugan and Gil Barker, a Deputy Comptroller of the Currency as well as Alex Sanchez the Executive Director of the Florida Bankers Association. Mr. Barker was the Assistant Deputy Comptroller in charge of the OCC's Tampa Office in 1992 when I joined FNBP.

It was Gil and his associates from the Atlanta OCC Office who told the FNBP's Board of Directors and me that the Bank was going to be closed. During our dinner in Miami, I reminded Gil that the OCC had said they were going to close the Bank, but they never showed up to close it. He said, "Lamar, I suppose enough time has gone by that I can now tell you why it was not closed." He went on to explain that the OCC's Office in Atlanta had made the decision to close the Bank but that he told them the Tampa Office had just approved a new President and that he asked them to give the new President a chance. They did, that new President was me.

Mr. Barker was promoted several times after leaving the OCC's Tampa Office. In 2017, as he was about to retire as Deputy Comptroller for the Southeastern part of the country, he was speaking at an FBA Conference in Miami. I was there and I enjoyed standing up and thanking Gil publicly for believing in me and giving the bank a chance to survive. That action on his part saved the bank from closing and probably saved my career. I think the industry needed more bank regulators like Gil during the great recession.

During my first year with First National Bank of Pasco in 1992, in addition to working with the regulators, I had to deal with the Bank and two of its officers being sued for $64,000,000. A Class Action lawsuit was filed in Philadelphia. The suit was due to the Bank having served as an escrow agent for what turned out to be a fraudulent transaction. The Bank was innocent of all wrongdoing because it did not know that its customer was involved in criminal activity.

Unfortunately, the bank did not have insurance to pay for its defense. We had to hire several Philadelphia Attorneys and I had to meet with them as well as FBI Agents in Philadelphia. We were successful in settling the case for about $250,000. This payment, plus the monthly operating losses the bank was experiencing, reduced the Bank's capital to about $1,000,000. In today's environment, that is not sufficient capital to keep a bank from being closed by the regulators.

That meant the bank had to raise more capital and that we did! It took one year, but we raised an additional $1,000,000 from local investors. The original 318,000 shares sold for $10 per share. The second offering of 318,000 shares sold for $3 per share. When I left the bank in 2009, I sold some of my stock for $25 per share. After I left, that price dropped to $9.

In April 1994, FNBP made its first profit and soon thereafter, the regulators removed the Consent Order restrictions. Over the next ten years the Bank's assets grew more than $100,000,000. It received Bauer Financials' highest five-star rating, and it became the second-highest performing community bank in Florida.

However, that did not mean that my leaving the bank in 2009 was a happy occasion for all concerned. It was not as I will explain later.

COMMUNITY AND BANKING INDUSTRY INVOLVEMENT WHILE IN PASCO COUNTY

While working on the bank's survival crisis, I also became very active in the community and later in the banking industry. Cindy and I were two of the organizers of the East Pasco Habitat for Humanity Affiliate. Neither of us was inclined to work on actually building a house, but we did enjoy the process of organizing the Affiliate, speaking at various churches and community meetings about it, setting up the accounting processes and, most importantly, raising the money to build houses.

We were organizing directors of the affiliate in 1993 and I served as its second president. Cindy was their volunteer treasurer until the organization grew to where it needed a full-time accountant.

By the end of 2018, that affiliate had built over 140 houses and had total assets of more than $2,750,000, mostly interest-free mortgages. All money received from the monthly payments on these mortgages pay operating expenses or invested in more houses. Its mission has always been to "build simple decent housing, giving those in need a hand up, not a handout." Equity for homebuyers is their sweat; they must help build their house or others that are under construction. They also must make the monthly, interest-free, mortgage payments as well as pay their taxes and insurance premiums.

I was also involved in the Dade City Chamber of Commerce and the Zephyrhills Chamber. In addition, I served on the Board and as Vice President of the Pasco Economic Development Board, the County Housing Board, and the Hospital Board.

From these involvements, I was recognized in two distinct ways. The Dade City Chamber of Commerce honored me as their "Business Leader of the Year" and the Zephyrhills Chamber honored me as their "Citizen of the year".

In 1999, John Wilburn, President of the Florida Independent Bankers Bank (FIBB) invited me to join their Board of Directors. FIBB was a unique bank, organized and owned by banks. It offered similar products and services as those traditionally provided by regional bank correspondent departments. FIBB was working through some problems, had just changed executive management, and was seeking additional Bank presidents to serve on their Board of Directors. I accepted, served six years on the board including one year as its Chairman.

Alex Sanchez, the Chief Executive Officer of the Florida Bankers Association (FBA) and I were having dinner one evening in about 2001. He asked if I had ever considered running for President of the FBA. I said, "No, but that it sounded interesting to me." He explained the process and I said I would discuss the possibility with Cindy, and my bank's Board of Directors. They both said, "Go for it."

I did and was successful, but it was not without challenges. Two Past Presidents of the FBA decided to support another banker seeking the position. My opponent was a very good banker and a friend of mine – still is. However, what the two promoters of my opponent did was not only unusual, but also misleading, unethical and, it backfired on them.

A letter in support of my opponent and appearing to have been signed by twenty-seven former Presidents of the FBA was circulated to the FBA's nominating committee. I was given a copy in an attempt to get me to withdraw from the race. The letter surprised me since I was friends with many of the bankers whose names appeared as signers on the letter. I called a few and they told me they had not signed a letter but had been contacted seeking their support for my opponent. They went on to say they did not know that I was seeking the nomination and therefore had given a tacit endorsement of my opponent. After I looked more closely at the signatures, they appeared very similar in writing style.

I brought this to the attention of a very well-connected banker asking him how I should handle this situation. I did not want to accuse those who had published the letter since it would look like "sour grapes". My banker friend said he would take care of it. He contacted all the members of the nominating committee and explained what had apparently happened. Later, I learned that the committee voted unanimously to nominate me and I was later elected by the association's membership.

Being able to serve as President of the FBA was a high point in my banking career. It gave me the opportunity to meet most of the bankers in Florida, as well as to travel to various FBA meetings in New Orleans, Seattle, Toronto, Montreal, New York, and Puerto Rico.

The travels also included many trips to Washington DC to meet with bank regulators and members of Congress. Often I would call my Congresswoman, Ginny Brown Waite, about joining me for dinner. Once, after she had accepted, she called back to say that the President had rescheduled his State of the Union Address and that she had to cancel our dinner plans to attend his speech. Then she surprised me by asking if I would like to attend. I immediately said yes. Then she asked whether Cindy would also like to attend. I told her that I usually did not speak for Cindy, but this time I would. Yes, she would want to go!

What a night, what an event! Sitting in the balcony of the Capitol with all those elected and appointed powerful people in the room below. Members of Congress, military leaders, Cabinet members, Supreme Court Justices, and the President and Vice President. Congresswoman Waite even arranged for one of her staff members to babysit Kaylie, our six-year-old granddaughter, in her office while we attended the event.

Once, when I was introducing my Congresswoman to a group of bankers, she told them that I had visited her office so many times that the security officers in her building would recognize me, and wave me through without any security check. That was not the truth, but it allowed the FBA members to know that I was looking after their interest in Washington, DC.

Cindy and I selected the El Conquistador Resort in Puerto Rico as the location for my FBA Annual Convention in 2005. The main speakers were Ben Stein and Dr. Ben Carson. I made my entry into the convention hall dressed as Elvis Presley. White jumpsuit, wig, and dark glasses. I had been portrayed as Elvis in a short video that the Association made about me. Each year such a video is made about the outgoing FBA President. They are always funny and lighthearted. The music for my video was from the Broadway play "Hair". In it, I wore several different wigs. Anyone can view this video on YouTube. Just type "Lamar Roberts, FBA" in the search window.

It shows me as I have never been seen before and will never be seen again!

**Lamar Roberts
2005 Annual Meeting Highlights**

21 Photo from FBA Annual Convention in 2005

During this same period 2000 – 2008, I became interested in and wanted to get involved with the Independent Community Bankers of America (ICBA), a trade Association that serves the community banks across the country, about 5000 at that time. I researched how to get on their Board of Directors and succeeded in being elected to represent all the community bank members in Florida on the ICBA Board.

While on the Board, I made friends with the Chairman-elect, who appointed me to the Board's Executive Committee as a Director-at-Large. There were only two such seats on the Executive Committee to represent the Board members from all 50 states. The other members of the Committee were either those in the Executive chairs (ICBA officers) or those who previously held those positions. Cindy and I enjoyed traveling around the country with this group at least once each quarter to attend their meetings.

As a member of the ICBA Executive Committee, I testified before a Congressional Committee. It was an honor to represent all the community banks in the country in front of the House of Representatives Financial Services Committee. Reading my prepared testimony was not stressful but knowing that the Congressmen could ask me any questions was. Fortunately, the questions they asked were simple.

My involvement with FNBP, IBB, ICBA and FBA meant we were on the go a lot of the time. In fact, I was out of the bank 182 days during one 24-month period.

Of course, there was a toll to pay. One morning, while on our treadmill at home, I had an unusual feeling in my chest. I stopped the treadmill and the feeling went away. I took a shower and left for the airport on my way to a meeting the next day in Miami. Alex Sanchez, FBA Executive Director, and I were meeting with the Board of Directors of the Florida International Bankers Association on the 30th floor of a high-rise office building on Brickell Ave. I was trying to convince them to merge with the Florida Bankers Association. While sitting across the conference table from these banking executives, having trouble understanding their foreign accents, Alex made a motion to me indicating that I should smile more. That is not something I do very often and particularly at that time because I was having chest pains.

The meeting ended without a decision. My chest pains subsided, and I flew back to Tampa that evening. The next day, I called my doctor to tell him about the chest pains. He examined me that afternoon, did not find any cause for the pain, but immediately sent me to a cardiologist who also did not find a cause for the pain. However, he told me to report to University Hospital in Tampa the next morning for a heart catheterization.

Cindy and Kaylie, our granddaughter, rode with me to the hospital the next morning. I was driving but I did not tell them that I was beginning to have chest pains again. I did tell the receptionist at the hospital and they immediately rushed me to the emergency room. Soon thereafter the catheterization began. As I was awakening from the anesthesia, the doctor told me I needed five heart bypasses. While being rolled out of the room, I saw Cindy and asked her if they had told her. She said, "Tell me what?" I said, "I have to have five heart bypasses." She said, "April fool". It was April 1, 2005. The nurse quickly told her that what I had said was not a joke!

A few minutes later, while in the recovery room, just after the catheterization, a doctor came in to tell me he was going to do my surgery. I told him to hurry up because I had to make a speech in Sarasota, on Monday, one in Dade City on Tuesday, another one in Orlando on Wednesday, and that Cindy and I had to be in North Georgia on Friday for an ICBA meeting. He suggested I get on the phone and cancel all of those engagements.

He reminded me it was late on Friday afternoon, that he had been operating since 6:30 that morning, that he was single, had plans for the weekend and he did not need my money. He then said, "They are going to make you comfortable upstairs in this hospital and I will see you Monday morning at 6 a.m. to do the operation. The bypass operation was performed on Monday, as planned.

I had some problems with atrial fibrillation after the surgery but was able to go home in about a week. Within twelve days of the surgery, I was back in the bank, and within 30 days, I was in Washington DC on ICBA business.

Going back to work only twelve days after the surgery was pushing it, but I thought the effort was necessary. I learned that my Senior Loan Officer had been working with the Chairman of the Board planning the Annual Stockholders Meeting. This was done without consulting me so I wanted to make sure that I was at that meeting.

My suspicions were confirmed. I learned that the Senior Loan Officer didn't think I would be able to return to the bank and continue as President and he thought he would get my job. That did not happen and our relationship was never the same.

One Sunday, while I was attending church, I received a call from another of the Bank's officers who told me that he had just found a note written by the Senior Loan Officer that said, "I hate my job." The next day, that Loan Officer gave me his resignation, and, during that week, I received resignations from the bank's Mortgage loan officer, Consumer loan officer, and Loan Administration clerk. We soon learned that the four of them were joining another bank that was opening an office located about a half-mile from our headquarters.

Losing those officers and the employee was a major setback for our bank, but we quickly adjusted to the turnover, filled three of the positions by promoting from within, and the fourth through the services of an executive search firm. The shake-up never affected our growth nor profitability. In fact, within two years the bank became the second-highest performing community bank in Florida.

When I joined the failing First National Bank of Pasco in 1992, I signed a simple employment contract that Greg Rains, my friend, and correspondent banker, helped me draft. The bank's attorney, who was also the founding and current Board Chairman, reviewed it and the Board approved it. It was a three-year contract that renewed each year unless either party decided not to renew. If either party decided not to renew the contract, on its anniversary date, it would be two years before it expired.

Other provisions included my original salary of $75,000, medical and life insurance for my family, a bank automobile and a bonus formula. I was to receive ten percent of the bank's profits each year that the bank made a 1% return on assets. Of course, at that time, the bank had never made a profit and the prospects of ever making a 1% ROA were very slim.

However, it did happen. Within a few years, I was receiving very lucrative bonuses, which by the time I left the bank in 2009, totaled about $1,500,000. My contract allowed me to use part of these bonuses to purchase stock in the bank at its current book value, which I did. Those purchases made me the bank's second-largest stockholder. In addition, the Bank had added a deferred compensation plan, a change of control provision, Bank Owned Life Insurance and a 401K plan to my benefits.

Over the seventeen years that I was with FNBP, the bank added several new Directors, who, obviously, were not on the Board when my original contract was negotiated. In 2007, under the influence of some of the new Directors, the Board decided that my contract should not be renewed, and therefore, I was put on notice that my employment would end in 2009. I naively thought they would change their minds since the bank was doing so well. Or, perhaps, they would agree to sell the bank and I could collect on my change of control payment.

To promote the sale of the bank, I introduced three investment bankers to the Chairman. They each told him that they thought the bank could be sold for about three times book value. The Board discussed this and decided they would hold out for four times book.

The Board appointed a three-man committee to review my contract and compensation. One of the members was upset that I was the second-largest stockholder, another disagreed with how my bonus was calculated, and the third said that he would never allow me to collect on my change of control payment which was three times my annual salary.

To make matters worse, the board voted to reduce my $177,000 annual salary to the $75,000 original amount that was in my contract. I informed them that my attorney said that could not be done because when they raised my salary, which they did almost every year, and the contract automatically renewed each year, the new salary took the place of the original salary. One Director then made this comment at a board meeting "that will be your salary until a guy in a black robe says otherwise." I said, "I think I can arrange that."

After my contract expired in May 2009, I sued the bank for back pay. Ultimately, we settled for an amount satisfactory to me. That amount, plus the amounts they paid me for various other benefits after I left the bank, totaled over $1,000,000. That made my wife, my attorney, our church, the IRS and me very happy.

Mr. Sumner was the main Director who orchestrated my split with the Board. His motive was to succeed me as President and he was successful. Within two years, under his leadership, the Bank was placed under a regulatory consent order and the value of the bank's stock dropped over 60%. He died shortly thereafter.

When I joined the First National Bank of Pasco in 1992, it had been in existence six years, had never made a profit, its capital was deficit, and it had asset quality and liquidity problems. It was under a regulatory consent agreement and the Directors were told the bank would be closed by the Bank Examiners

When I left in 2009, the Bank's assets had grown $ 100,000,000.It had no asset quality problems, had excess capital, was paying stock dividends and offering to buy back shares from holders who wanted to sell theirs, was the second-highest performing community bank in Florida and had no problems with the regulators. Its Bauer rating was Five Stars, the highest rating given any bank in the country.

The following pages contain an article about my leaving the Bank that was published in the Tampa Times Newspaper. While being interviewed for the article, I decided not to disclose what the Bank's Directors tried to do to me to get me to quit and not to disclose the false statement made by Board member, Bobby Sumner. There are untruths in it but I refused to "wash the bank's dirty laundry" in the press.

Pasco Times

tampabay.com

Sunday, April 12, 2009 | PAC

Murky split for bank, leader

First National's president says he's baffled that board wants him out.

BY HELEN ANNE TRAVIS
Times Staff Writer

DADE CITY — When J. Lamar Roberts took over as president and CEO of First National Bank of Pasco in 1992, he was known as a financial Mr. Fix It.

The bank's reputation was not so hot.

At the time, First National was losing money and had a growing pile of problem loans. Federal regulators had urged the board of directors to find new management and tighten up its lending habits.

Fast forward 17 years to a time when bank failures and bailouts are common fixtures in the news, and you'll find First National sitting pretty.

The bank is one of 22 among 310 state banks to recently receive five stars — the highest rating — from Bauer Financial, which rates banks on how well-capitalized they are in an era of higher loan losses, among other criteria.

First National is the only Pasco County bank to earn Bauer's "superior" status. The second highest rated is Lutz's Heritage Bank of Florida, which earned four stars and an excellent rating.

First National's rate of non-performing assets (technical speak for overdue loans) is a tenth of the average for the Tampa Bay area, according to the accounting firm Saltmarsh, Cleaveland and Gund.

"First National, they're a solid institution," said Bill Massey of the firm's financial institution advisory group.

From sinking to "solid," you would think the bank's board of directors would be quite happy

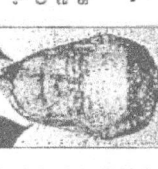

J. Lamar Roberts, 67, helped the bank move out of a dismal period when he took over in 1992.

with their presidential pick 17 years ago.

But Roberts, who had planned to stay at the bank until his retirement, is job hunting. His

» See BANK, 7

contract with First National expires April 20.

Robert Sumner, president of the bank's holding company and the only board member who could be reached by the *Times*, said the board and Roberts could not reach an agreement on his contract.

"The bank board, having a history of conservative posture, and in this type of economy, we just were not able to resolve the issues," he said.

He did not elaborate.

•••

Roberts, 67, is quick to share the bank's success with its 41 employees, the community and customers.

Under his oversight, the bank developed its current lending strategy. First National gives loans mostly on commercial, owner occupied real estate, single-family dwellings and its "niche market," retirement homes in upscale senior mobile home parks.

The bank avoided subprime loans and lending to developers.

"That is, from my perspective, speculative lending," Roberts said.

"Lamar Roberts is one of the most meticulous people I've ever seen," said Nathan Botts, a shareholder at Saltmarsh, Cleaveland and Gund. "Many bankers call on him for advice when they get in trouble."

•••

Roberts keeps a photo in his desk of his childhood home in Troup County, Ga., where five people shared three rooms. The outhouse was in the back yard, the hand crank well in the front.

The son of a minister, Roberts was drawn to banking because "they have air conditioning, and you get to wear a coat and a tie."

His resume has come a long way since his first $1 per hour teller gig.

At 29, he was president of a bank that became one of the best performing in Florida.

In 1988, *Florida Banking* magazine wrote a glowing article about Roberts called "Pride of the Panhandle," when a Fort Walton Beach bank's assets more than doubled after seven years under his watch.

Roberts was also president of the Florida Bankers Association between 2004 and 2005.

His record of recognition and success make the bank board's decision to let him go all the more baffling. But Roberts isn't giving any more details about the separation — and neither is Sumner, the holding company president.

The reason for the split is staying secret — at least for now.

First National's board has not yet found a replacement for Roberts, who, as expected, already has several job options lined up.

The financial fix it wizard said leaving the bank will be "one of the saddest days in my life," but adds he holds no grudges against the board.

"I don't understand what they're doing, but I accept it."

Helen Anne Travis can be reached at htravis@sptimes.com or (813) 435-7312.

Chapter Eight – 2009-2011

FIRST NATIONAL BANK OF CENTRAL FLORIDA

While trying to enjoy my forced retirement, I started calling my banking contacts around the state looking for an employment opportunity. One friend, Debbie McKillop, the CFO of the First National Bank of Central Florida in Winter Park said, "The Bank, where I am working is having problems with its asset quality and dealing with the regulators. You might want to talk to our Chairwoman and CEO to see if she would consider having you join our team."

I had met the Chairwoman once at an FBA Convention, so I called her to suggest we have lunch. She agreed, and while we were dining, she asked why I wanted to meet with her. I said that I knew her bank was having problems and I wanted to see if I could help. She knew I had experience and success in working in similar situations. At first she hesitated but later agreed that maybe I could help. The President of her bank said he would give up his position to me and that he would become the bank's Chief Operating Officer. As it turned out, he gave me his resignation while we were having lunch, the first day I reported to work.

The Chairwoman and I agreed on an employment contract and their Board of Directors approved it. At the first Board meeting that I attended, the bank examiners from the Office of the Comptroller, OCC, presented the Board with a Consent Agreement that the board was required to sign. The examiners already had a line for my signature, so I had to commit to manage the bank according to their requirements and the standards set out in the Consent Agreement This was similar to the situation I previously dealt with at First National Bank of Pasco.

For the next year, we worked together trying to understand the Bank's problems, what caused the problems, and how to correct them. The bank needed $25 million in additional capital to absorb the losses they had to take and remain adequately capitalized. I told this to the patriarch of the family, the chairperson's brother, who lived in England. I asked him if the family had that much liquidity, and would they use it to recapitalize the bank. He said they did have the money and that they would make that additional investment before they would let the bank fail.

The family had originally bought a minority interest in the bank. With the additional capital they later had to invest, the family then had a total of about $38 million invested and had become the bank's majority shareholder. The Chairwoman was of Indian descent. She was born and raised in England where she was educated as an attorney. When she was in her mid-twenties, she moved to the USA. During the next several years, she worked in the bank, attended a Graduate Banking School and eventually became its Chairwoman and CEO.

Because, at that time, the country was in a great recession, there was little demand for the real estate developments the bank had financed. The loan customers could not develop or sell the property, and the bank could not foreclose and sell the land without incurring very large losses. Ultimately, the Chairwoman's family had to decide if they were going to invest/risk the additional capital the bank needed to survive. They decided not to do that. As a result, the OCC and the FDIC closed the bank on May 6, 2011. Once again, I had been retired against my will.

I would not wish that experience on my worst enemy. Although I was not supposed to know when the bank would be closed, I found out through my contacts. I knew the date and time, as well as the identity of the bank that won the bid to take it over. That did not make it any easier. It was like waiting for a firing squad to arrive. It was embarrassing and awkward to have government officials tell you to hand over the bank's charter, your door keys, and your bank credit card. Armed police officers stationed at each door and in front of the vault made sure bank staff was not stealing anything. It was both sad and humiliating.

Usually, the closing of a bank by the regulators marks the end of a bank executive's career. However, I was one of the fortunate bankers who got another chance to manage and successfully turn around a bank that was required to hire an experienced "crisis manager."

RMPI CONSULTING (RISK MANAGEMENT & PROCESS IMPROVEMENT SPECIALISTS)

In June 2011, one month after the First National Bank of Central Florida closed, I attended the Florida Bankers Association's Annual Convention. It was a little embarrassing to be there with my peers because they knew what had just happened to the Bank where I had been President. However, community bankers are some of the best people to have as friends and acquaintances. No one made me feel uncomfortable.

During one of the coffee breaks, I met David Brown, the managing partner of RMPI Consulting. I had heard of the company and talked to a couple of their consultants earlier that year. Mr. Brown told me in detail about the services his company provided for banks, most of which were dealing with regulatory issues and asset quality challenges. His background and that of his associates made them a good choice as consultants to help banks comply with regulatory Memorandums of Understanding and Consent Agreements.

He said he knew of my background and that I had recently been President of the Florida Bankers Association. He was also aware that I knew many community bankers in Florida, and he thought I could help them solicit new business as well as be a consultant for them, particularly with their executive coaching and strategic planning services.

After several more meetings, and after completing my due diligence on their company, I agreed to join them as a Principal. For the next several weeks, I traveled with Mr. Brown throughout Florida visiting banks that might need our services.

Chapter Nine – 2011-2019

FIDELITY BANK OF FLORIDA NA

In July 2011, I received a call from Jack Greeley, a highly respected bank attorney whom I had known for several years. He had been the attorney for First National Bank of Central Florida as well as for the Florida Independent Bankers Bank. Jack said, "You might be getting a call from Fidelity Bank of Florida in Merritt Island. They are looking for a new CEO and I recommended that they talk to you."

Later that day, I received that call from the bank's major shareholder. I knew a little about the bank. It had been very successful, growing rapidly, making above average profits, and had higher than normal capital and reserves. It had one of the state's highest net interest margins and one of the best efficiency ratios. However, it had the reputation of making loans differently than most of its peers and funding the loans with above-market interest rates paid for certificates of deposit.

He told me that he had resigned under regulatory pressure and that the Board had been required by the OCC to hire a crisis manager. The OCC also told the Board that the Bank was subject to being closed because of its unsafe condition and noncompliance with their Consent Agreement.

The handwritten notes that I took during that conversation, which I still have, records him saying that the bank would pay me an annual salary of $250,000 and I would be given $5million in bank stock once the bank "turned around."

I followed up that call by arranging a meeting for David Brown and me to meet with the Bank's President and another Board member. That meeting went well and I later met with the other board members. At that meeting, I learned that the bank already had a consultant, but that they were not pleased with his work nor his results.

Later, Mr. Brown and I met with the board and I told them that I was a Principal with RMPI and that initially, I would only work with the bank as an RMPI consultant, and afterward, perhaps, as its CEO. I further explained that for me to work for them initially, it would be necessary for the bank to contract with RMPI. RMPI and I would do what was necessary and could be done to comply with the Consent Order and return the bank to a safe status. The Board accepted RMPI's proposal. We later learned that the other consultant had resigned.

The contract that RMPI signed with the bank called for me to be a consultant and the bank's "acting CEO", subject to OCC approval. The OCC approved my temporary position as acting CEO immediately, while they were considering approving me as the permanent CEO. That approval came on January 31, 1992. I then stopped being a consultant and became the bank's CEO. This resulted in a reduction in my income, since as a consultant; I was receiving a percentage of RMPI's billings plus $200 per hour for my services as a consultant.

My personal employment contract with the bank was negotiated at the same time as the one with RMPI. It was to take effect once the OCC approved me as the bank's Chief Executive Officer (CEO). We agreed on a $250,000 annual salary, life, medical, disability and dental insurance, director fees and six weeks paid time off for vacation or sickness and a $1,000 monthly automobile allowance.

Because I lived in the Tampa area and would not be relocating my family to Brevard County, I also requested that they provide me a furnished, two-bedroom, two-bath, condominium on the beach of my choice, with the bank paying all related expenses, including maid service and utilities. They agreed. I chose a condominium unit five buildings south of the Cape Canaveral inlet where the cruise ships pass and within sight of rocket launches from the Space Center. I stayed there four nights a week for over eight years. That was one of the most unusual benefits I have received as a Bank Executive. It proved to me that "it does not hurt to ask and if you do not ask, you usually will not get."

My first instruction from the OCC was to terminate the current President. I asked if I could just demote her instead. They reluctantly agreed but said that she could not be an Executive Officer or a Director. It was hard for me to tell her about all of this. After trying out her new position as the Bank's Branch Administrator for a few weeks, she resigned and then sued the bank for wrongful termination and sex discrimination. Eventually, the plaintiff withdrew the lawsuit without any consequences to the bank.

Below is a paper I wrote about my eight years at Fidelity Bank of Florida. I think it captures the condition of the bank when I joined it, what our team did to save it, and the results we achieved.

WHY FIDELITY BANK OF FLORIDA NEARLY FAILED

By J. Lamar Roberts

December 2018

Background and History

A local attorney organized Fidelity Bank of Florida in 1990. He was Chairman of the Board and CEO from 1990 to 2010. He has always been and is now the bank's majority shareholder. The bank also has about 150 minority shareholders. Its first office was in Merritt Island, and over the years, two more offices were added one in Longwood and another in Port Richey, Florida. I closed the Port Richey office in 2012.

During its first 15 years of existence, Fidelity Bank was one of the fastest-growing, most profitable, highly capitalized and most efficient banks in the state. In March 2008, the Bank had assets of $438,439,000 and equity of $54,104.000. However, when the recession hit later that year, the business plan the Bank had been operating under resulted in asset quality problems, operating losses, and insufficient capital. In addition, the business plan fell out of favor with the bank's regulator.

By 2010, it became apparent that the Bank was a troubled institution. It appeared that it had gotten into this condition by operating as a wholesale bank rather than as a traditional community bank. The bank's loans were funded with local certificates of deposit paying above-market interest rates, wholesale certificates of deposit, and fixed-rate, Federal Home Loan Bank (FHLB) advances.

Loan brokers, to whom the bank paid a referral fee, produced a large percentage of the loans for the bank. The loans were in 42 states and were heavily concentrated in convenience stores and hotels. Only minimal underwriting information was documented. The main qualifying factors for loan approval appeared to be an indicated large equity in the real estate pledged, and the customer agreeing to pay an above-market interest rate. Financial information was only required for the initial approval, none thereafter. There was no viable system to confirm that insurance coverage remained current, that taxes were paid or that loan payments were made on time. In addition, there was no requirement for loan customers to become depositors of the Bank. Therefore, as of December 31, 2011, only 1.4% of the bank's deposits were demand deposits, as compared to its peer average of 7.95%.

Regulators had consistently criticized these practices but had never required that they be changed prior to the 2008 recession. At that time, OCC placed the bank under a Memorandum of Understanding, which was not fully complied with either. Therefore, the bank was required to sign a very strict Consent Agreement, which was also not complied with. The Chairman of the Board and CEO resigned in December 2010.

In September 2011, the bank contracted with RMPI, a bank-consulting firm out of Boston, Massachusetts, to assist in complying with the Consent Agreement and to staff a temporary Special Asset Department (SAD) with consultants. J. Lamar Roberts, a principal with the firm, received immediate approved from the OCC as the bank's acting CEO. He became the Bank's President and CEO in February 2012.

These stats indicate the bank was "sick" and might fail.

	2008	2009	2010	2011
Net Income	($3,528,307)	($11,388,28)	($26,502,40)	($3,250,323)
Provision Expense *	5,730,087	18,600,152	27,868,503	6,014,357
Loss on Sale of ORE **	547,908	3,323,407	2,576,922	246,123
Loss on Sale of Securities	15,615,103	716,193	0	0
Allowance for DTA***	0	0	8,787,792	0

* Allowance for loan and lease losses
** Other real estate owned (foreclosed property)
*** Deferred tax asset

A sick Bank's condition can be diagnosed in a similar manner as a sick person's condition. For example, doctors use symptoms and blood workup norms while bank regulators use peer comparisons and regulatory norms.

Below are stats from the Federal Financial Institutions Examination Council's (FFIEC) Uniform Bank Performance Reports. It compares Fidelity Bank to its peer averages in 2011 and 2018.

		12/31/2011		9/30/2018	
		FBFNA	Peers	FBFNA	Peers
Capital					
	Tier One Capital	4.11%	9.40%	13.75%	11.53%
Asset Quality					
	Nonaccrual loans	19.19%	2.79%	0.06%	0.64%
Earnings					
	Interest Income	5.80%	4.50%	5.01%	4.26%
	Interest Expense	2.51%	0.90%	0.81%	0.61%
	Net Interest Income	3.28%	3.60%	4.21%	3.64%
	Noninterest Income	0.00%	0.70%	0.09%	0.45%
	Noninterest Expense	2.54%	2.93%	3.08%	2.74%
	ALLL Provision	1.64%	0.53%	-0.19%	0.08%
	Net Income	-0.88%	0.67%	1.05%	1.15%

Fidelity Bank's sicknesses could be diagnosed as "Cancer," "Obesity," and "Anemia" as described and explained below. The bank did not, nor does it now, have any problems with liquidity or regulatory compliance.

Cancer

Non-performing loans, excessive liquidity, and a mismanaged investment portfolio caused the "cancerous condition".

The treatments, between 2012 and 2017 for the "cancer" included:

- Eliminating $56,000,000 in non-performing assets (NPA). Approximately, $31,000,000 of these NPAs were returned to accrual status increasing interest income by about $1,860,000 per year.
- Foreclosing on 182 properties and then selling them for $20,743,257, which resulted in losses and cost totaling $6,051,000 plus legal expenses of $4,324,000. At one time, the bank had 122 foreclosures active at the same time being handled by 32 different law firms. Later the bank had to contract with a management company to operate four hotels it owned in two states and hire an attorney to coordinate the attorney's efforts.
- Charging off $17,745,000 in uncollectable loans during the period 2012 to 2018. From 2008 to 2011, the bank had charged off an additional $53,929,000.

By December 2018, either the $56,000,000 in non-performing assets were returned to accrual status, charged-off or foreclosed and sold. This eliminated all NPA, except for $380,000. There were two sale contracts pending on these parcels for $409,000.

These "treatments" cured the bank's "cancer."

Obesity

The "Obesity" was caused by an excessive, $70,000,000 fed funds sold position, a $50,000,000 FHLB advance and $53,000,000 in wholesale deposits.

The $70,000,000 in fed funds were earning 0.25%. That liquidity had accumulated as loans paid down or paid off. New loans were not being made and the excess funds were not being invested in securities or used to shrink the bank. In the fourth quarter of 2011, $50,000,000 of the fed funds were invested in Government National Mortgage Association securities (GNMA) earning 2.25%. This 2% difference increased the bank's income $1,000,000 per year. In the second quarter of 2012, a bond swap of these investments resulted in a gain of $1,292,000 making the bank profitable in June 2012 for the first time since 2007.

The $50,000,000 invested in GNMA securities could have been used to pay off the $50,000,000 FHLB advance, which had a fixed interest rate of 5.3%, except that by doing so the bank would have had to pay an $8,100,000 prepayment penalty. With only recent and marginal profits and a 4.11% capital ratio, (the regulators were requiring that the bank have a 9% capital ratio), the bank could not afford to absorb that penalty. In addition, the 2.5% interest income ($1,125,000 per year) from the GNMA investments was insufficient to cover the 5.3% interest cost of the advance, $2,650,000 per year. In other words, a negative arbitrage of $1,525,000 per year existed.

To find an answer to this dilemma, the services of an Investment Banking firm in New York City were retained. They said that if the bank's CPA and the Regulators would approve, the bank could restructure the advances from a fixed rate to a floating rate advance reducing the interest cost from 5.3% to Libor plus 25 bps floating. The $8,100,000 prepayment penalty would have to be paid. However, with the proper approvals, it could be capitalized and written off over the life of the restructured advance. That would reduce the bank's total cost for the advances to 3.3% (interest plus amortization of prepayment penalty) and would reduce its interest expense by 2%, $1,000,000. per year. The approvals were obtained, the restructuring was accomplished, and the savings were realized.

This greatly improved the situation until interest rates started rising increasing the interest cost on the advance because of its floating rate structure. In addition, the GNMA investments and the FHLB advance were a strain on the bank's capital. They were unnecessary assets and liabilities on the balance sheet since the bank had adequate liquidity without the GNMA investment, and the bank was not making loans. By eliminating both the GNMA and the FHLB advances, the bank's net interest income would increase and the capital needed to support them would be reduced $4,500,000 (9% of $50,000,000). Therefore, a decision was made to sell the GNMAs and pay off the FHLB. However, this action required that the unamortized portion of the prepayment penalty be expensed. Fortunately, in 2016, the bank was strong enough to sustain that expense. The after-tax cost of the charged-off prepayment penalty balance was $1,862,000 and a $163,000 profit on the sale of the GNMA reduced the net effect on capital. After shrinking the bank by $50,000,000 and expensing the pre-payment penalty, the bank's Tier One Capital ratio increased from 9.3% in 2015 to 11.48% in 2016 and its pretax income increased $750,000 per year.

The bank's "obesity" was further reduced by using the cash from pay downs and payoffs of loans to reduce the bank's wholesale certificates of deposits from a high of $53,000,000 to $7,539,000 freeing up the need for the $4,770,000 capital needed to support those liabilities.

Other steps taken to reduce the bank's "obesity" included:

- Closing the Port Richey Office, which was only producing Certificates of Deposit that paid above market interest rates. Closing this office reduced operating expenses $100,000 per year.
- Reducing interest rates on core certificates of deposits as they matured and renewed
- Not making any loans for four years.

These "treatments" cured the bank's "obesity."

Anemia

The "anemic" condition refers to the bank's insufficient capital.

Many of the steps used to treat the "anemia" are listed above. Others included:

- Shrinking the bank's balance sheet by $200,000,000 over a five-year period, which reduced the bank's capital deficiency by $18,000,000. (9% of $200 million)
- Reducing all cost associated with the Special Asset Department
- Reversing $250,000 of the ALLL's unallocated balance back into capital.

These 'treatments" resulted in the bank becoming profitable in June 2012, the first time since 2007, and the bank's Tier One Capital ratio improving from 4.11 % in 2011 to a current ratio of 13.11% This capital could support the bank growing its assets by $120,000,000 without having to raise any additional capital. That growth could increase after-tax profits by $1,200,000

These "treatments" cured the bank's "anemic" condition

Two major adjustments to the bank's equity were made during this seven-year period:

- The first was the elimination of the $13,240,000 reserve against the bank's differed tax asset (DTA) when it was no longer required. This entry increased the bank's equity by that amount, but not its Tier One Capital. The bank's Certified Public Accountant, (CPA), decided, in 2013, that this reserve was not needed. This was because the bank had demonstrated that it could and would continue to operate at a profit and that the Deferred Tax Asset would be used to offset future tax liability.

- The second was a $4,552,000 reduction in the Deferred Tax Asset when the combined effective tax rate for the bank was reduced by Congress from 37.7% to 25.1%, December 31, 2017.

Stats and Facts:

Cost of the Fidelity Bank of Florida turnaround, 2008 – 2018

- Charged off 853 loans totaling $71,674,000
- Consultants to deal with the OCC Consent Order and develop a Special Asset Department charged $1,762,000
- Appraisals for OREO, Trouble Debt Restructured (TDR) and classified loans totaled $750,000
- Loss and cost (other than Attorney fees) associated with foreclosed real estate added up to $16,712,000
- Attorney fees were $4,324,000
- Charge off of Freddie and Fannie preferred stock amounted to $16,331,000
- The total cost was $111,553,000.

Other Stats of interest

- Reduced staff from 47 to 33 employees
- Reduced past-due loans from 24% to 0.33%.
- Reduced criticized assets from $104,500,000 to $400,000.
- Increased earnings from a ($3,250,000) loss in 2011 to projected profit of $1,750,000 in 2018.
- Reduced out of state loans from $51,191,900 to $7,200,000.
- Reduced OCC and FDIC expense from $1,859,804 in 2011 to $116,795 in 2017.
- Increased insurance coverage for the bank and reduced premium expenses over $250,000 per year.
- Paid dividends totaling $658,282 in 2017 and 2018.
- Increased market value of the bank from zero in 2012 to $32,500,000 in 2018.

Other factors existing at 12/31/11

- Net unearned Financial Account Standards Board (FASB) fees of $3,176,184, were accreted into income, as loans were paid off or charged off.

- Allowance for Loan and Lease Losses (ALLL) balance 12/31/11 was $16,334,000. No additional allocations to the ALLL were required since June 2012.
- High rates on loans, 5.8%, 97 percentile to peers.
- High cost of funds, 2.51 %, 91 percentile to peers.
- Low net interest income, 3.28%, 26 percentile to peers
- Stockholders capitalized the bank with approximately $3,500,000 in 1990. The sale of additional shares in 2010 increased the paid in capital by $3,400,366.

Without these factors, the bank's survival would have been less likely.

In addition to "curing" the diseases, so the bank would survive, other improvements were needed for the bank to transition from a Wholesale Bank to a Community Bank. These goals and objectives included making Fidelity Bank a good place to work, a good place to bank and a good place to be a stockholder. To accomplish these objectives, the following steps were taken:

<u>New products, services, benefits or departments</u>

- Mortgage Department
- Marketing Department
- Human Resources Department
- Treasury Department
- Special Asset Department (later disbanded)
- GLAD Department, Getting Loans And Deposits (business development department)
- Small Business Administration Loans (Certified Lender and Preferred Lender status achieved)
- Nationwide ATM Network
- Internet Banking
- Mobile Banking
- Remote Deposit Capture
- Bill Pay
- Fun Committee for employees
- Wellness Committee for employees
- Employee monthly newsletter
- 401K plan for employees
- Incentive and bonus plans for employees

- Loan Portfolio Managers
- Loan Analysts
- Internal loan reviews
- Loan exception tracking
- Financial Statement tracking
- Expired insurance tracking and force-placed insurance issued

<u>Improved, facilities, products, services, benefits</u>

- Two new electronic marquees installed
- Longwood Office interior renovated and decorated
- Merritt Island Office upgraded
- Two new semi-private offices built in the lobby
- Cubicles for loan administration installed
- Renovated offices for Senior Loan Officers
- Renovated and decorated Board Room
- Core Processor upgraded to Horizon, all computer hardware was upgraded, servers moved to highly- secure Peak 10 location, IT and Information Security support were outsourced and the IT staff was reduced by two.
- Retained Bank Legal Counsel at less than 50% market rate (he coordinated 32 law firms handling 122 lawsuits at one time)
- Five new Directors were recruited and elected
- Implemented Director orientation and training program
- Improved Director Board reports
- Expanded Director committees
- Improved ALCO information and presentations
- Created the Enterprise Risk Committee and policy
- Installed Financial Compass software to improve budgeting and financial accounting.
- Revised and updated all policies and procedures
- OCC Consent Order removed
- Improved regulatory ratings and relationship
- Achieved Five Star Bauer Rating (rating in 2012 it was "0")
- Voted Best Financial Institution in Merritt Island twice
- Selected as Chamber of Commerce, Business Champion of the year
- Improved community involvement – Outstanding CRA rating at last exam

- Upgraded Strategic Planning process and plan
- Updated and improved the Bank's Website
- Installed Salesforce CRM program to track sales efforts
- Improved insurance coverages and choices for employees
- Set up escrowing for taxes and insurance
- Electronically imaged all loan files for loans larger than $250,000
- Provided continuing banking education to all employees, Compliance Officer earned two Professional Designations, Certified Regulatory Compliance Manager (CRCM) and Certified Community Bank Internal Auditor (CCBIA), Senior Lending Officer Graduated from the Graduate School of Banking at LSU, Marketing Director received, Master Social Media Certification, Retail Manager received Human Resource Management Certificate, others completed bank-related College courses and attended industry training conferences and schools
- Reduced loan accounts without insurance from approximately 50% to zero
- Reduced loans with unpaid real estate taxes from approximately 75% to zero

How was this Crisis Management challenge approached, tackled and accomplished?

Prayer

That is why some call the saving of the bank a "Miracle"

"accepting the things we cannot change, and changing the things we can."
Partial quote from the Serenity Prayer

Planning

Strategic plans

Goals

Action plans for each department

Incentives paid for results

Organizing, deputizing and supervising

Communicating, educating and motivating

People

Ever improving, capable, experienced, educated and dedicated officers and staff

Supportive Board of Directors (one was a retired Assistant Director of the OCC who had supervised Fidelity Bank)

Consultants, the first responders who stabilized the bank until the appropriate staff was hired

The right people in the right job at the right time. Some needed initially were not needed long term

Good working relationship with regulators

Correspondent bankers, who helped restructure the investment portfolio and establish Asset Liability Management (ALM)

CPAs, advice, recommendations, and approvals

Attorney, highly rated, Washington DC-based, community bank Attorney who also had represented ICBA for 38 years and 400 community banks across the country

Policy and procedures.

All reviewed and rewritten to be appropriate for the new community bank

Patience, persistence, and perseverance

NOW, THE REST OF THE STORY!

The main duties and responsibilities of a Bank's Board of Directors include hiring the CEO, making sure management is operating the Bank in a safe and sound manner, assuring that management is responding to regulatory concerns, and representing shareholders' interest in protecting and increasing their investment. This includes selling the Bank if it is in the shareholders' best interest.

As it turned out, dealing with insufficient capital, poor asset quality, criticized management, large loan losses, lack of operating profits and not being in compliance with the OCC Consent Order were not the most frustrating and difficult challenges faced by the Board and bank management. It was dealing with the majority shareholder, who was the Bank's previous Chairman and CEO. He criticized, abusively, nearly everything that was being done to save the Bank.

I could understand the OCC's frustration and strong tactics they used to get the Board's, and particularly the Chairman and CEO's, attention about the bank's condition in 2009, 2010 and 2011. After reading the 2010 and earlier Reports of Examination, it was apparent that the Bank Examiners' reaction to the bank's poor condition was not only just based on the recession that was adversely affecting most banks, but rather to the lack of positive response from the Bank's Chairman. The regulators were harsh on the Directors and management because they were not responsive to the original Memorandum of Understanding or the more recent Consent Order. The OCC's only remaining remedies were to remove executive management or close the bank. The Chairman and CEO resigned in January 2011.

While the OCC's actions, in my opinion, were warranted and necessary, the majority shareholder-former Chairman's attitude and actions towards the board and new executive officers, especially me, were not. The former Chairman, who was also an attorney and the organizer of the bank, was being investigated by OCC for mismanagement and was prohibited from entering the bank building or contacting bank officers. However, his wife remained a member of the Board of Directors.

The OCC's investigation resulted in the former Chairman being required to sign a personal Consent Order and pay a fine. He blamed his Board of Directors for not supporting him in the investigation and accused them of throwing him "under the bus" to protect themselves. I did not find that to be the case.

During the first couple of years I was with Fidelity, I had very little contact with the major shareholder. The OCC had told him not to come into the bank building nor have contact with the employees or officers about bank business. He did call me one time shortly after I had joined the Bank. During that call, he questioned some of my actions and made suggestions. I thanked him for recommending me for the job but told him that if I were going to run the Bank **I would have to do it my way.** He replied politely, "Perhaps we should not talk." I responded politely that I would be glad to talk to him as a shareholder anytime, but I would be making the decisions of how the bank would be run. I offered to resign if he wanted to find someone else. He did not respond to that comment.

Over the eight years I was with the bank, I only met with him a few times. None of those were pleasant meetings and none changed the way I managed the bank. It was apparent to me that it was very difficult for him to have been removed from the CEO and Chairman Position and not be involved in the management of the bank. I could understand him feeling that way but I could not and would not let him disrupt the progress we were making.

The OCC required that the Bank's president be terminated or demoted and removed from the board. When this was accomplished, she sued the bank for discrimination based on gender and retaliation. She later withdrew the lawsuit.

Other Directors told me that the OCC said the bank would need $15 to $18 million in additional capital to keep it from being closed. The Bank did raise about $3 million in additional capital in 2010 but could not find investors willing to purchase more. The bank's capital needs and were later mitigated by its return to profitability in 2012 and by the new management team strategically shrinking it assets $200 million.

After the former president left the Board, only the regulatory minimum of five members remained. About a year later, one of the five remaining Directors gave notice that he planned to resign. I asked the Directors if they knew of any shareholder or potential shareholder they would recommend as a new Director. They did not. It was difficult for me to ask anyone to join a board of a bank in a troubled condition. Directors assume fiduciary responsibility for the Bank's condition and, under certain situations, may be personally liable for losses the FDIC incurs if the Bank fails.

In 2013, while attending a shareholder meeting of another bank, I visited with Ken Page, one of its Directors. Ken was a retired Assistant Deputy Comptroller of the OCC. and had been in charge of regulating all national banks in South Georgia and northern Florida, including Fidelity Bank. It was while he was supervising Fidelity, that the bank was required to sign the Consent Agreement.

I asked Ken if he would consider joining our board, and he surprised me by accepting. His advice over the next several years was very beneficial in helping the bank's officers and directors comply with the Consent Order. He also provided a regulator's view on asset-liability management, the investment portfolio, loan underwriting, and regulatory relations.

Shortly after Ken joined the Board, another Director resigned. In order to find a replacement, I spoke with leading businessmen and professionals in the Merritt Island area and asked for recommendations. Several suggested local businessman Tom Weinberg. I met with Tom, told him what being a director of a bank involved, and answered his questions. He said he had never been a Bank Director but would enjoy learning and doing his part.

Mr. Weinberg's family has lived in Brevard County for three generations. He had held executive positions in state and county governments and had served as Chief of Staff for one of Florida's US Senators, who had been on the Senate Banking Committee. When Tom joined our Board, he was the Chairman of the Cape Canaveral Port Authority, a prestigious position. It quickly became apparent that Tom was a fast learner and the right person for the job.

In 2012, the bank had 122 active lawsuits pending (mostly foreclosure actions) and 32 different law firms were handling these cases. In order to better and more efficiently manage this caseload, I recommended, and the Board approved, hiring Len Rubin as the Bank's General Counsel. Mr. Rubin was a well-known community bank attorney with 40 years' experience. He had just retired from a prestigious national law firm in Washington DC where he managed their bank regulatory practice. During his career, he represented more than 400 community banks throughout the country and successfully sued the OCC on regulatory issues on behalf of community banks.

I met Len when he was outside General Counsel for the Independent Community Bankers of America (ICBA), whose members were the nearly 5000 community banks in the country. Len was ICBA's General Counsel for 38 years. His responsibilities for Fidelity were to oversee and manage the 32 lawyers working for us, as well as to advise the bank on regulatory compliance matters and corporate governance. We were very fortunate to have him agree to work with a bank that was struggling to stay open.

The backgrounds of these key people are included here because they were particularly instrumental in our efforts to save the bank. They all assisted in returning the bank to profitability by resolving asset quality problems, increasing the bank's capital ratios, managing interest rate risk, strategizing how to shrink its assets and liabilities, and improving the bank's CAMELS rating so the Consent Order could be satisfied. They are also mentioned here because the majority shareholder required that these three resign, or not stand for reelection to their positions with the bank before he would agree to vote on the sale of the bank. This will be explained later.

The Consent Order was satisfied and removed by OCC, November 9, 2015. Shortly thereafter, several investors approached Fidelity about the possibility of purchasing the bank. One investor offered a less than market price and the Board declined the offer. That investor then approached the majority shareholder with an offer to buy his shares and the shareholder signed a simple agreement to sell his majority shares to the investor. During the following 12 months, the Board learned that disagreements had developed between the shareholder and the investor concerning the validity and enforceability of that agreement, so no action was being taken to pursue a final sale.

During that same period, another unsolicited offer was received from a financial institution offering a reasonable purchase price for 100% of the bank. The Board thought that the offer should be considered and was in favor of pursuing negotiations. When the majority shareholder learned of this, he sent a letter to the Board saying he was not interested in selling the bank at that time. However, the Board felt that it had a fiduciary obligation to pursue an offer that it believed was in the best interest of all shareholders. Therefore, at my suggestion, the Board contracted with Nick Barbarine, a leading investment banker with Hovde, to advise the bank on responding to the offer.

The Board believed that the majority shareholder would not consider the new offer because of the sale agreement he had previously signed. They asked the Chairman of the Board to send a letter to the majority shareholder advising him that the Board believed that this offer was in the best interest of all shareholders, but that they would not continue to pursue it unless he agreed in writing to vote his shares to approve the sale. He refused, and the offer had to be rejected.

During this time, 2017 – 2018, the majority shareholder expressed his concern, indirectly, that he was not being consulted on certain actions taken by the Board. The shareholder apparently did not know that the Board had no obligation to consult with any shareholder prior to taking action. Frustrated and angry, the shareholder decided to take action at the December 2017 Annual Shareholder Meeting by attempting to remove, (by not reelecting Ken Page,) a director whom he believed consistently disagreed with him. The shareholder made a motion from the floor to reduce the number of directors from eight to seven and then, presumably, he would vote for all but this one objectionable director.

After receiving advice from our General Counsel, I ruled the motion out of order because, among other things, the proposal to reduce the number of directors was not included on the proxy statement sent to all shareholders, and thus they were not given the opportunity to vote on the matter. The shareholder's vociferous reaction to my ruling disrupted the meeting to the point that I was forced to adjourn the meeting and continue it the following month. During that 30-day period, in an attempt to mollify the majority shareholder, the bank's Articles and Bylaws were revised to clarify how Directors would be elected and how the number of Directors would be determined.

When the 2017 Shareholder Meeting reconvened in January 2018, all of the existing eight directors, including Ken Page, were reelected, and the shareholders, including the majority shareholder, approved the proposed changes to the Articles and Bylaws. However, shortly thereafter, the majority shareholder advised the Board that he was still unhappy with the process for electing directors and wanted the Articles and Bylaws changed again. In a further effort to appease the majority shareholder, the Board and bank counsel tried to rewrite them several times. The majority shareholder twice met with the Board continuing to complain about the redrafting of the Article and Bylaws, particularly the language concerning voting methods. Each time the Board offered to consider any rewrite he wanted to propose. No proposed changes from the shareholder were ever received.

CENTRAL FLORIDA EDUCATORS FEDERAL CREDIT UNION (LATER RENAMED ADDITION FINANCIAL CREDIT UNION)

In 2018, after the Board had to decline an earlier purchase offer, it received an unsolicited Letter of Intent from the Central Florida Educators Federal Credit Union (CU), headquartered in Lake Mary, Florida. The CU's Letter of Intent stated a firm interest in buying the bank and included a proposed price, subject to due diligence. After review and after receiving advice from its investment banker, the Board believed that this offer was in the best interest of all shareholders and counter-signed the Letter of Intent. The due diligence was performed and was satisfactory to the CU.

In order for a sale to be finalized, the Bank's shareholders must approve it. That meant that the majority shareholder must agree in writing to vote in favor of approval. The majority shareholder told the Board that he would approve the sale on one condition: that directors Page and Weinberg and General Counsel Rubin resign. He singled out these three individuals because they consistently opposed actions proposed by him and his wife, a Director. These two directors and the general counsel said that they opposed the shareholder's proposals because they were either unwise and/or not in the best interest of all shareholders and/or contrary to regulation and proper corporate governance. Although the demand by the majority shareholder was clearly just his revenge for their opposition to his actions, all three gracefully agreed to resign because they knew that the sale was in the best interest of all shareholders. In January 2019, the Board formally accepted the CU's $32;500;000 ($74.06 per share) offer and the shareholders approved the sale in April 2019.

During one of the majority shareholder's meetings with the Board, he asked Chairman, Janson Davis, a question. When Mr. Davis did not give the answer the shareholder wanted, the shareholder threatened to call a special meeting of shareholders to remove Mr. Davis from the Board. The shareholder subsequently filed a request for a Special Shareholders Meeting, as he had a right to do, but withdrew it before the Board acted upon it when he was told that the Credit Union might reconsider their offer if Mr. Davis was removed from the Board. There was also the possibility that other Directors might resign which would put the bank in violation of the required minimum of five Directors.

It became apparent that the major shareholder was attempting to remove anyone from the Board or management who did not agree with his wants and wishes. He obviously planned to nominate new Directors who would follow his lead. While he was successful in removing some of those he did not like, not all of those he nominated to replace them became his puppets. Some were very good, independent thinking Directors who represented all the shareholders very well.

Mr Davis, the Board Chairman that the majority shareholder was threatening to remove from the Board, had been an organizing Director and had served on the Board since November 1990. He had been responsible for bringing and refereeing more deposits to the bank than any other director, officer or shareholder. He reluctantly accepted the Chairman position in January 2011, when the OCC forced the majority shareholder to resign. Janson had worked diligently with me over the years. He is a successful business owner, a major supporter of the bank, and a true gentleman. He has served on several other Bank Boards and is well known as a community leader. His advice is frequently sought by young and old alike, wealthy businessmen and those just starting a business. His advice and counsel were critical to the success of my work to lead the bank through its crisis and survival.

The majority shareholder withdrew his action to remove Janson from the Board on the condition that a Special Shareholder Meeting be held to again vote on approving changes to the Bank's Articles. This would put them back to the way they were prior to December 2017. The board agreed and retained outside special counsel to redraft the documents and call a Special Shareholder Meeting to approve the changes. Under the circumstances, with a sale of the bank pending, the exercise made no sense but was accomplished simply to appease the majority shareholder.

This meant that three months before the merger with the Credit Union was scheduled to close, a Special Shareholder Meeting was held to change the Bank's Articles and Bylaws back to how they were in December 2017. Of course, none of this was necessary because of the pending sale; the shareholders would never have an opportunity to elect Directors again using the revised Articles and Bylaws. Therefore, the $120,000 plus in legal expenses incurred to accomplish this and the other actions of the major shareholder were unnecessary . . . money wasted.

After the merger, I accepted the CU's offer to assist them with the transition through the end of 2019. My retirement at that time would be one month short of the first day I started working in a bank, 60 years ago, February 1960.

When I started working at Fidelity Bank in 2011, the Bank's stock had no market value. No one would make any additional investment in the Bank to keep it from closing and no one could find buyers for the shares they wanted to sell. In the eight years that I managed the Bank as President and CEO, the Bank's value increased from $0 to $32,500,000, $74.06 per share, which is what the CU paid. In addition, over the 30 months prior to the sale, shareholders received $1,097,138 in cash dividends, $2.50 per share.

As mentioned earlier, in July 2011, the majority shareholder called to ask me if I would accept an offer to become CEO of Fidelity. During that conversation, he said the OCC was requiring the bank to hire a "Crisis Manager" and he knew that I had experience with troubled banks. I asked, "What is in it for me". According to my handwritten notes (that I still have), he said: "How about a $250,000 salary and $5 million in bank stock?"

I decided I should get the $5,000,000 stock offer in writing. To accomplish this, I wrote the shareholder the letter shown on the next page.

It only seems like a few weeks ago, instead of a few months ago, when I received the fateful calls from each of you. Boy, what a difference a few months make. As you might recall, my first reaction was surprise and a lack of interest in the CEO position with your Bank. I had not gotten over my last losing battle with the OCC but the idea of returning to Brevard County was intriguing. Especially when you mentioned that you would give me $5,000,000 in Fidelity Bank stock if I accepted the offer.

I initially came thinking the OCC might not approve me, or that it was too late to save the Bank or that I would not stay more than three to six months. Therefore, I did not mention or think much about your promise until recently.

Now, I believe the Bank can make it. I am enjoying the challenge and I am considering staying for the duration. This brings me to the reason for this email.

Reducing your generous offer to a written agreement could help seal my decision. I believe it can be done without creating a regulatory problem. In fact I believe any such agreement should be prepared by competent counsel and a copy given to the OCC for their review.

Are you willing to put your offer in writing?

I look forward to receiving your reply and continuing to accomplish the challenge you have given me.

Lamar

22 *A copy of the letter I sent the Fidelity Shareholder.*

The next day, I received a phone call from him in which he said that no such offer or promise had ever been made. The following day, the shareholder's wife, a Director, said, "Mike says he will give you 20,000 shares of Bank stock if the bank turns around and survives. However, we are not willing to put that promise in writing."

In August 2013, while I was meeting with the shareholder's wife again, I asked if the offer of the stock was still good. She said that it was. I told her that she had specified nothing except the number of shares. In addition, there was no date set for the transfer of the stock, or what I would have to do to receive it. She replied, "When the Bank turns around, you will receive 15,000 shares' (note that the number of shares offered this time had dropped from 20,000 shares to 15,000. I did not point out the difference).

In March 2019, four years after the Bank "had been turned around," I again asked the shareholder's wife when I would be receiving the stock. She replied that her husband had changed his mind about giving me the stock because he believed that I had been paid enough for what I had done. Nothing else has ever been said about the stock offer and of course, I never received any of the shares promised.

Fortunately, Cindy and I will have a comfortable retirement. However, not as good as it would have been if I had received the $5M in bank stock or the 15,000 shares, now worth $1,110,900, that was promised. The majority shareholder's family received over $22 million because the bank survived and was sold.

This experience reminds me of Moses who led the Israelites through the wilderness for forty years but was not allowed to enter the Promised Land. I was privileged to lead Fidelity Bank from being an undercapitalized, unprofitable, doomed bank to being a highly capitalized, profitable bank that was awarded the highest bank rating in the country, but I was denied the reward that had been promised.

However, this did not stop me and our team from making the bank a safe and sound, very profitable financial institution which was a good place to work, a great place to bank and a terrific investment for its stockholders. The results are shown on the next page.

RESULTS

In 2010, Fidelity Bank's Bauer rating was "0". In 2018 and 2019, it was rated 5 Star.

Bauer Financial is a nationwide bank rating company that rates every bank in the country using public regulatory financial information. No banks pay for the service and banks cannot avoid being rated... Ratings are from "0" to five Stars.

SUCCESS

Success might be defined differently by the person seeking it as compared to others who are observing and judging it. My favorite definition is "The progressive realization of worthy goals." To me, it is not just fame or fortune, but also how one accomplishes goals measured from where one starts to how far they have progressed. I believe it should include health and happiness as well as how much one has helped others. The best thing that can be said of a person at their funeral is that "The world is a better place because of the life we are celebrating."

I feel successful because of where and I began my life's journey and where and how I am now, at the end of my career, as I eluded to in the prologue of this book, I was not to the manor born. We always had food, clothes, and shelter but not much more except our love for each other and God. I never made excellent grades and never earned a college degree. However, as described earlier I did pursue higher education over a twelve-year period after graduating from High School.

So, why was I able to become a Bank Executive at a young age and hold similar positions over my sixty-year career? I believe it was because of how I dealt with the people I came in contact with: my parents, teachers, fellow employees, supervisors, bank customers, bank board of directors, bank examiners stockholders, voters, community leaders, peers, politicians, spouse, and children. To be successful one needs to be liked, trusted, respected and perhaps revered. I learned that a lot depends on how you make other people feel about themselves and how they feel about you. They rarely care how much you know until they know how much you care.

The best lessons I learned on how to do this were taught in a Dale Carnegie Course. The lessons were based on a book written by Dale Carnegie titled "How to Win Friends and Influence People. Here is an outline of those lessons.

> Never criticize, condemn or complain
>
> Show sincere appreciation
>
> Make people feel wanted
>
> Be interested in others
>
> Smile
>
> Call people by their names
>
> Talk in terms of their interest
>
> Listen attentively
>
> Make others feel important

I am not an expert at any of those but I did try to act them out.

Many years ago I read that we should try to visualize two little signs pinned to everyone's chest. The first would say "Make me feel important" the second "What is in it for me." Thinking of those wants, as we talk to others, will help us address them positively.

I had my first paid leadership position during my Senior Year in High School. I was teaching, leading and conducting Adult Church Choirs. All of the choir members where older than me and they were all volunteers so I could not make them do anything. I had to make them want to do what I was asking and to feel good about it.

My second paid leadership position was as a department head in a bank. I was twenty-two years old and all of my employees were, once again, older than me and had more experience than I did. Therefore, my approach to leading them was treating them as if they were volunteers and trying to make them want to do what was I was requesting and to feel good about it. Of course, that does not always work. There are those that want to show you they do not have to do what you are requesting. Those I sent home. I always tried to treat unpleasant situations with "medicine" first, i.e. words, if that did not work, I treated it with "surgery," i.e. removed them from their positions.

There are times to stand up and times to shut up. It is an art to know the difference. If we do not stand for something, we might fall for anything. A leader has to respectively consider other people's opinions, but also be decisive. It can be detrimental to just go along to get along. However, a leader should also consider changing his mind if new facts are presented that he did not know when making his first decision. Also, they should admit being wrong when that is the case.

During my career as a leader, I made many mistakes, none were fatal but many were embarrassing and sometimes costly. I tried to turn those mistakes into learning experiences.

A successful leader must have a vision, be able to get his followers to "buy into his vision" and follow him. A leader must also have "managerial courage," removing team members who are not doing their job satisfactorily or who have a bad attitude that is distracting others. Bad attitudes are contagious and can spread. They must be addressed and corrected. It has been said that people with bad attitudes have "stinking thinking and need a checkup from the neck up for hardening of their attitude." Research has shown that more people are fired for having a bad attitude than for their aptitude.

Successful leaders must also be good planners and time managers. To best manage my time, I used what I call the "Four D" method. When any paper or decision hits my desk I either, Do it, Ditch it, Delay it, or Delegate it.

Strategic Planning was my method of deciding what needed to be done to accomplish the bank's goals and objectives. Here is the outline of the process I used.

- SWOT Analysis shows the Bank's
    - Strengths
    - Weakness
    - Opportunities
    - Threats
- Mission Statement (Why are we here)
- Vision (What you want to become)
- Values Statement (For what do we stand)
- Objectives (What do we want to stop, start, change or improve)
- Goals (should be measurable in time, dollars, numbers or percentages)
- Action Plans (Who will be in charge of doing what by when) (monthly or quarterly reports should be made for each goal and objective)

I found it very important to plan your work and then work your plan.

Chapter Ten

IT IS NOT ALL ABOUT ME

While this book was being edited, I was reminded that I had written it all about me. Who I was, where I came from, what I did, where I went and what I accomplished. I responded "Sure" that was my intent. I was then told, "You did not do all of that without help from others." That was also an accurate observation.

My parents encouraged me and gave me everything they could. My brothers were there when I asked for or needed help. Cindy was always supportive and generous with her good advice and suggestions. My employers took a chance when hiring me and giving me opportunities to grow and learn. My teachers and professors did the best they could with what they had to work with and friends comforted me when I messed up, made mistakes or experienced setbacks. I had mentors who I admired even when they did not know that I was learning from their examples and that I wanted to be like them. There were others that I wanted to make sure I was not like them because they had bad character traits, were not honorable, honest or trustworthy.

However, the greatest guidance, instructions, encouragement, and hope I ever received came from God and the Holy Bible. He was always there for me even when I was not seeking or doing His will. There were times when I left his presence but He never left me or let me down. He was always there when I turned to Him and prayed for his help, wisdom, forgiveness, mercy or grace. Without him, I could not have done anything. So, I say "To God be the Glory for the great things He has done." I feel I have been truly blessed. I led two Banks from threatened closure to safe and sound conditions, high ratings and outstanding performance. They were miracles in my opinion, and we all know where miracles come from: Our Heavenly Father.

MY GREATEST GIFTS, JOY, REGRETS, AND HOPE

Some of the gifts, for which I am the most thankful, include my life, my liberty, my family, my friends, my health and my happiness. However, the GREATEST gift was my salvation, which was made possible by God's gift of his Son, Jesus Christ and Jesus' gift of His life for the forgiveness of my sins.

To receive that gift all I had to do was accept Jesus as my Savior, confess my sins and strive to live a "Christ-like" life. This did not make me perfect because "all have sinned and come short of the glory of God" but it did assure me that at my death I will go to heaven to be with Him and all other believers who have predeceased me.

My greatest joy came from helping others, either by example, teaching, mentoring, coaching, befriending or giving. For years we have deposited a percentage of our income in an account for charity or to help others. The rest was deposited into our regular account to pay our bills or be invested. Cindy and I believe that our gifts for "charity and others" has accounted for much of the financial success with which we have been blessed.

My greatest regrets include the sins I have committed and the hurt I have caused others.

My greatest hope and prayer is that everyone who does not know Jesus will make His acquaintance, accept Him as their Savior and follow His teachings as taught in the Holy Bible. I believe that those who do will go to Heaven at their death and that their life on earth will be filled with Jesus' love, mercy, and grace. All of these come with our accepting Him as our personal Savior and having faith in Him.

- His Love gives us comfort and joy.
- His Mercy can save us from the punishment we deserve for our wrongdoings.
- His Grace can give us rewards we did not earn or deserve.
- His sacrificial death on the cross paid for our sins.

It is very simple. The Bible says, *Believe on the Lord Jesus Christ, and thou shalt be saved....* (Acts 16:31, KJV).

Who could ask for more?

Appendix

The following pages contain articles and items of interest from throughout my life.

PRESIDENT'S MESSAGE (FIDELITY BANK'S WEB PAGE)

Thank you for visiting our website. On it, you can better get to know Fidelity Bank and find the products and people to meet your financial needs.

We are a community bank serving Brevard County from our office in Merritt Island and the Orlando area from our office in Longwood, FL. In fact, our market area actually extends throughout the I-4 corridor. You will notice that our services are designed for individuals of all ages as well as for small to medium-size businesses of all types. We pride ourselves in offering both **high tech and high touch** products and services.

When you have a financial need or question, please contact us by phone, email or come into one of our offices. A directory of our officers and contact personnel, with their direct lines, is included on this website. This directory will help you contact the right person who is waiting to serve you. Of course, you can always call our main number (321) 452-0011 and a real person, not a computer, will answer your call and make sure you are connected to the person or department that can meet your needs.

Please read our "**World Class**" service pledge that all of our employees have signed. We take this pledge seriously!

You are always welcome to call me. My direct number is (321) 328-1414. I answer my own phone and if I cannot take your call immediately, I will see that it is returned within 24 hours.

We are honored to have many satisfied customers. Additional customers are always welcome.

Sincerely,

J. Lamar Roberts President & CEO

ARTICLES WRITTEN ABOUT ME:

BANK SUCCESS STORIES

A Bank Is Only As Good As Its Bankers

Understanding the power of good people has made a huge difference to the management success of one Florida community bank.

William A. Hamilton and
Penny R. Hamilton

AT FIRST BLUSH, one might conclude that J. Lamar Roberts is reserved, courtly, impeccably dressed, compulsively neat, and obsessed with order and organization. All true. Up to a point.

J. Lamar Roberts, the president and CEO of First National Bank & Trust of Ft. Walton Beach, Florida, is all those things, and more. Roberts may understand more about human potential and its development than any bank president in the United States. Moreover, Roberts has used his enormous people skills to make First National one of the nation's leading community banks.

But the story of Lamar Roberts, like that of First National's principal owner, James J. Tringas, is not one of being to the manor born. Roberts, the son of a Baptist preacher, was raised, as he puts it, "in a Georgia farmhouse with a path instead of a bath."

Tringas, the son of a Greek immigrant, worked days running a retail business and nights running a movie theater. By 1956, Tringas was in a position to become one of the founding investors in First National.

Both Tringas and Roberts are fiercely independent. About a decade after the founding of First National, some of Tringas' fellow investors wanted to sell the bank to outsiders. Committed to local ownership in community banking, Tringas gained control of First National and became its chairman. Today, First National is owned by Southern National Banks, Inc., a one-bank holding company owned by the Tringas family and the bank's ESOP.

Roberts describes his relationship with Tringas, whom he met and got to know at several international banking seminars, as somewhat akin to that of father and son. His relationship with John Tringas, the bank's vice chairman and head of marketing, is like that of a brother.

Promoting the American Dream

Ask Lamar Roberts if every staffer at First National has a chance to make it to the top and he will hand you a set of career flowcharts. He has a separate chart for tellers, secretaries, clerks, bookkeepers and proofers. Each chart shows a career path leading from entry-level position to senior management.

From the teller's seat to the executive suite, Roberts is dedicated to the idea that the skills needed to continue the success of First National can be developed in-house. "Promote from within is not a bunch of hype at First National," says Roberts. "It's been four years since we had to go outside the bank to fill an officer slot."

The ability of First National to promote from within rests, in large measure, on how the bank selects its personnel and upon First National's "College of Banking."

"The Tringas family and I are big believers in education," says Roberts. "We hire winners or potential winners to begin with and then afford them continuing professional education in banking. By helping them maximize their potential, we keep personnel turnover low and build a real spirit of 'family' within the bank.

Dress for Success

STAFFERS in most banks present a nice appearance to the public. But, at First National, everyone, from bottom to top, is dressed for success. Indeed, the staff looks like a mini-convention of well-heeled investment bankers. On commercial bank salaries, "the look" is hard to attain, so First National assists employees with an interest-free "dress-for-success" loan.

"Our College of Banking has two main purposes: it enhances on-the-job performance and it prepares our staff for advancement within the bank," says Roberts. First National's College of Banking is conducted in conjunction with Okaloosa-Walton Junior College, which, in turn, hires many of First National's senior staff as instructors.

"Our staff knows we take continuing education very seriously," says Roberts. "While the entry program is mandatory for all employees, the intermediate, advanced and graduate programs are optional. With James Tringas serving as chancellor, myself as president, and the bank's executive vice president, J. Larry Beasley, as dean, I think the staff understands the importance of continuing their education."

First, Know Thyself

But continuing education is not the only way Roberts measures development. Each officer is required to complete a self-evaluation each quarter with the rest of the staff participating in and receiving annual evaluations. These self-evaluations are based on performance standards or goals as mutually agreed upon by each subordinate and each supervisor.

The self-evaluations are one-third of a three-part system used to determine the amount of an employee's bonus. The bank's ROE, plus supervisor evaluations, form the other two legs of the bonus-determination triangle.

As a result of the evaluation process, the top 15 percent, the "high performers," are identified. It is from this group that the bank expects to find its future leadership. Eighty percent fall into the category of "stable performers," with the remaining 5 percent identified for special assistance. Those in the bottom 5 percent are not eligible for raises and are expected to react to the rating system in one of two ways: respond positively to counseling; or seek another line of work.

Round Pegs: Round Holes

At First National, searching for the best extends into personnel selection as well. However, if a bank employee does not do well in a job assignment, Roberts' initial assumption is that the bank, not the employee, has erred.

That assumption rests upon First National's hiring and job assignment process — a process that begins with a comprehensive personality test. For example, First National's loan department needs, to use Roberts' terminology, "finders, minders, binders and grinders."

Finders are loan officers coached and encouraged to find, not discourage, borrowers. Binders are underwriters. Their job is to scrutinize prospective loans and make recommendations as to their performance potential.

Minders are those who service the loans and perform other accounting functions. Grinders have the task of ensuring that poorly performing loans are paid off.

Specific Aptitude

Roberts feels these various tasks are best performed by people who show an aptitude in specific areas. Rarely does his test-driven selection process misfire. But, when it does, he goes back to the data.

Most often, it is just a matter of transferring the staffer to what the tests show as his or her second-best aptitude area.

Roberts preaches the gospel of goodfinding. "Catch somebody doing something good and praise them for it," Roberts urges his officers. But inherent in goodfinding is the expectation that each individual will work diligently to attain his maximum potential. Roberts sees one of his main duties as the removal of obstacles to individual achievement. Or, to use Maslow's term — self-actualization.

It would be difficult to imagine the kindly, courtly Roberts chewing out a staff member. Indeed, in this highly charged "ever-upward" environment, an expression of disappointment by Roberts is much more effective and long-lasting than a harsh word.

Mindful of Helping Hands

Roberts' enthusiasm for helping others up the ladder is rooted in his own past. Beginning with menial tasks in the fourth grade, Roberts has always had to work. His first steady job was running a cash register in a grocery store.

One day, a church deacon asked him what he wanted to do with his life. Since he liked wearing a suit and tie and the local bank had air-conditioning — an important consideration in the Deep South — Roberts said he would like to work in a bank.

A week later, the deacon returned with news of a job opportunity at the local bank. The grocery job and the banking job each paid $1 an hour; however, Roberts could see more opportunity in banking.

By working part-time at the bank as a teller and teaching church music part-time, Roberts supported himself through college. Following his freshman year, he worked full-time in the bank during the summer. But, in the fall, he continued to work full-time while enduring a 100-mile daily commute to college and back. His bank augmented his $200-per-month salary with money for books and tuition.

By age 20, Roberts was making loans. At 21, he was assistant cashier and a department head. By age 24, he was named assistant vice president. He went on to complete the Georgia Banking School at the University of Georgia and later became a graduate of the Graduate School of Banking of the South at Louisiana State University.

Young Success

In 1965, Roberts moved to Florida where he became cashier of a $3 million bank. By age 26, Roberts was elected mayor and a city judge of his new hometown. When he was only 29, he became a bank president.

Then came the presidency of Florida National Bank of Brevard County. Following that, Roberts was promoted to be in charge of loan review for Florida National Bank — the statewide bank holding company.

During that time, Roberts renewed his friendship with James Tringas, who asked Roberts to become president and CEO of First National Bank & Trust of Ft. Walton Beach.

Yearning for the chance to become, once again, directly involved with community banking, Roberts accepted.

Since then, First National has seen steady growth — a growth resting on John Tringas' marketing skills and Roberts' talent for organization and human resources development.

The Senior Folks at Home

Keenly aware of Sun Belt demographics, the Tringas family and Roberts initiated special programs for the bank's senior customers. "Suite 100" is a deeply carpeted and richly paneled suite of offices just off the main lobby which is always available to "high-balance" customers. Patterned after the special club facilities offered by the major airlines, "Suite 100" provides a quiet and serene banking environment for customers with balances above a certain level.

A specially trained staff caters to the needs of customers entitled to use "Suite 100." This concept has worked so well that First National has spun off another set of special services for its "51st Club" — a club composed of senior customers regardless of bank balance. The staff of "Suite 100" administers the "51st Club" as well.

Whether senior customer needs have to do with estate planning or merely rolling over a CD, they are handled with the dignity and decorum and, above all, the respect the bank feels senior customers should be accorded.

Roberts, for all his emphasis on personality testing, free continuing professional education, bonus programs, clothing loans, awards and special handling of senior citizens, is no patsy. He is a steely-eyed taskmaster with his eye on the bank's bottom line which is just fine.

We Did it Our Way

INNOVATION and creativity at First National are not limited to human resources development. Being different, and above all independent, is a long tradition at First National.

Even before J. Lamar Roberts was brought to the bank by James J. Tringas in 1981, the bank had been doing its own data processing by writing its own software and running it on Unisys hardware.

In time, it became apparent that a better software solution was needed and an outside software vendor was chosen. But, recently, when that software vendor delivered an ultimatum that First National must switch to another brand of hardware, First National's traditional independence asserted itself, once again.

Turning to his chief financial officer, J. Larry Beasley, Roberts commissioned a search for a new software vendor that would support Unisys hardware. The search ended with the selection of Information Technology, Inc. (ITI).

"Larry Beasley gave us his typical outstanding performance in selecting ITI," says Roberts. "In fact, we are so pleased with our conversion to ITI software that our bank has taken the lead in forming an ITI user's group for this part of Florida and the Southeast. Our nature is not only to be fiercely independent but to lead as well.

"Our data processing staff has a long history of innovation so we like the flexibility of ITI's parameter-driven system. It means we can ask for and get enhancements to what is, in our opinion, the best integrated data processing system in the financial services industry.

"When it was just a $72 million bank, First National had 112 employees. Today, at $160 million, we have added only six new employees and that includes staffing a new branch bank. Clearly, our in-house data processing capability has enabled us to grow while holding personnel costs in line," says Roberts.

"I try to hire people who are smarter than I am," says Roberts. "Frankly, we have any number of jobs I cannot do as well as the people in them.

"My job is to hire the very best people we can and then see to it that they get the very best professional training plus all the tools they need to excel."

The pursuit of excellence is clearly the name of the game at First National Bank & Trust of Ft. Walton Beach — a game that is being won each day, not only in terms of human resources development but in ROE and ROA as well. ■

William A. Hamilton and Penny R. Hamilton are free-lance writers who live on Lake Branby in Grand County, Colorado.

FEATURE

Pride of the Panhandle
Lamar Roberts Leads First National Bank With a Steady Hand

By Paul M. Thompson

J. Lamar Roberts has taken First National to $163 million in assets.

Finders, Binders, Minders and Grinders. No, it's not your newest local law firm. They are the affectionate job descriptions J. Lamar Roberts uses for his team of banking professionals at the First National Bank & Trust of Fort Walton Beach. Finders are commercial officers (salespeople paid a salary plus commission), binders are underwriters (officers with loan approval authority), minders handle loan servicing, and grinders—you guessed it—deal in that wild world of collections.

The unconventional titles solicit a laugh or smile from visitors but they speak volumes about Lamar Roberts and explain why, after he took over as President & CEO of First National in 1981, the bank has increased assets from $71 million to $163 million while expanding to five branches and 129 employees.

The bank was organized in 1956 by a group of local businessmen who thought the Fort Walton Beach area needed a national bank. A minority shareholder and director, Jimmy Tringas believed in the originating group's idea that the bank should be locally owned and operated and within ten years of its origination, Tringas took control of the bank and has served as its chairman ever since.

His son, John Tringas, is vice chairman of the board and heads up the marketing arm of the bank. The Tringas family owns Southern National Banks, Inc., a one-bank hold-

(CONTINUED ON PAGE 10)

(CONTINUED FROM PAGE 9)
ing company which owns most of the bank's stock. The bank's ESOP is the second largest stockholder.

Roberts brings the best of two world's to the bank leadership. On the one hand, he is a highly-disciplined—some may say rigid—administrator. He'll reach into the credenza behind his desk and pull out a black, 5-inch-thick procedures manual. "This is how we run our bank," he says flatly. Or he'll whip out the bank's five-year plan, carefully documented with action plans tied to individual responsibilities tied to employee incentives developed by his executive vice president, J. Larry Beasley.

Then, Roberts takes you into his other world, where the emphasis is on the personal development of the bank's employees. It begins with a personality profile to determine what area of the bank a person is most likely to be most effective. It follows with intensive in-house training, much of it on video-tape. And it continues to the College of Banking that Roberts helped create exclusively for First National employees at Okaloosa-Walton Community College.

"Our people are what make us different—we think better," says Roberts. "So much of what banks offer in terms of products and services is the same. Good people providing good service can make the difference."

It's that attitude that has helped First National increase profits every year in the 1980s despite increased competition within and outside the banking industry. "We've had six new banks open here in the last two to three years plus we compete with the largest military credit union (Eglin Federal) in the country," says Roberts.

According to Roberts, the outlook for banks in Fort Walton Beach depends primarily on three factors: military growth (Eglin and Hurlburt Air Bases are both located in the area), tourists and new industry. And right now, only the military is expanding with the move of the 23rd Air Force to Hurlburt Field. Tourist spending is off because Fort Walton Beach is so dependent on visitors from economically depressed Louisiana, and attracting new industry has been difficult especially when the competition is incentive-oriented Alabama just a few miles away.

In addition, the real estate market is soft and what major activity has taken place is often by out-of-state developers. Growth is problematical because Fort Walton Beach is locked in by the ocean and the Eglin reservation, the largest Air Force Base in land size in the free world, larger than the state of Rhode Island. But the uncertainties of the local market have not kept the bank from remaining profitable.

In fact, only the area's over-built situation and the accompanying decrease in property values have knocked First National below the 1.5 percent earnings on assets mark that was categorizing it as a "high-performance" bank.

Roberts has always related to "high performance." He is one of Florida banking's fast-tracking high-achievers. Twenty-eight years ago, he started his banking career in Georgia, the son of a Baptist preacher, and earned $1 an hour as a teller. At 20, he was loaning money, at 21 a loan officer, at 22 a department head, and at 29 a bank president.

"When I began lending money in 1960, they gave me a scratch pad, a pen and a set of blank promissory notes and told me to talk to the applicants – 'look into their eyes' to see if they were credit-worthy," recalls Roberts. "We did not have application forms or credit files, nor were we even members of the Credit Bureau. Everything back then was calculated by hand. We paid two percent on passbook savings and four percent on CD's and we loaned money at six percent. Things have changed."

Indeed they have. But Roberts enjoys banking more than ever today in the deregulated environment. "It's tougher but it's more fun," says Roberts. "It used to be a simple game of attracting interest rate-regulated deposits on which we were virtually guaranteed a profit. Now, we look at deposits as inventory we must control and invest at a profit. Today, we're asset-driven with new products and services. It's been especially challenging for community banks but I think we're proving we can hold our own."

On the issue of new products and services, Roberts would prefer banking remain "pure." But since other industries have encroached on banking's turf, banks need the power to move into securities, insurance and real estate. "We have the credibility with the customer, and the customer would benefit if we could serve them in new and better ways," says Roberts.

Roberts serves his own profession as a leader of the Florida Bankers Association. This year, he's a member of the FBA's governing council, an associate director of the FBA School of Banking, and a member of the Community Bankers Committee. He is heavily involved in professional education and especially proud of First National's College of Banking.

The bank pays Okaloosa-Walton Community College to conduct the courses and the college pays the instructors, most of whom are First National Bank officers, and coordinates all the educational activities, including graduation ceremonies. The four-level program ranges from entry level courses like business ethics and corporate culture all the way up to a graduate program when employees tagged for senior management positions learn the intricacies of corporate finance.

At First National, education is just part of developing the total bank professional. The bank's human resource officer offers career counselling and employees are even given an interest-free payroll deductible allowance advance to purchase the kind of clothes that allow them to present the best possible appearance consistent with their responsibilities at the bank.

If you walked from department to department within First National Bank, you would feel a vibrancy created by an organization of well-trained, motivated, efficient professionals. Walk into the president's office, and you have arrived at the source.

J. Lamar Roberts

July 28, 2014

Fidelity Bank of Florida, N.A., in Merritt Island, Fla.

J. Lamar Roberts
President and CEO
55 years a community banker

Fidelity Bank of Florida, N.A.

- Merritt Island, Fla.
- $268 million in assets
- 42 employees
- Two retail locations
- Founded in 1990
- www.fbfna.com

As I write this column on my desktop computer, whose data files are brimming with reports, regulations and procedures, I think back on my first day as a community banker in 1960. My desk held a supply of blank promissory notes, a pencil and a scratch pad to manually calculate interest. Daily entries were made by hand in a leather-bound journal.

"Back in the day," loans were made without application forms or credit reports. We wrote a note, shook hands, disbursed the funds and followed the most important rule—know your customer. After all, it only took 19 years for me to be faced with the first foreclosure of my career.

Five decades later, it would be impossible to make such loans. In the 1960s I earned my pilot's license and flew low over cattle ranges to count heads of cattle collateralizing a loan. Today, they'd just tattoo a bar code on the cattle and get three reports per day.

http://independentbanker.org/2014/07/j-lamar-roberts/ 8/6/2014

The passage of time and advancement of technology has made banking both easier and harder. It is this constant change which has made my career a combination of challenging, frustrating and, most importantly, rewarding.

One of my early mentors told me the three ways to collect loans. "Trick it out of them or love it out of them, and if all else fails—cuss it out of them." His underlying point was simple and has not changed in all this time. Every customer is unique and the secret to being a good banker is to find out how to work with, and for, your customer.

I entered this industry 55 years ago as a dollar-per-hour teller, and was promoted every year until being named president at age 29. That doesn't make me special, but it shows how much this industry has changed. The fact my first annual salary as president was $14,400 tells even more about change over time.

During the course of serving as president of six different community banks—three of which became the highest-performing banks in Florida—I've seen the introduction of branch banking, drive-up windows and ATMs, and the unveiling of APR, APY, RESPA, CRA, ACH, ALLL, ALCO, BSA and CAMEL (and then CAMELS). While working as a community banker, I served as both mayor and municipal judge in a small town and was arrested and briefly jailed while driving a repossessed car with an expired tag. My ownership of an insurance agency on the side enabled me to afford to have a career in banking.

Along the way, serving as president of the Florida Bankers Association and on the ICBA Executive Committee were an immense privilege. In 2011, I undertook improving a bank under a regulatory order, and just two years later we led all community banks in Florida in return on average equity.

I would not trade my career in banking for any other. Today I walked into my office filled with the same enthusiasm as my first day on the job in 1960. As long as I feel this good about it, I'll keep showing up every day.

ARTICLES WRITTEN BY ME

| BEST PRACTICES

PERSONAL WELLNESS

J. Lamar ROBERTS

J. Lamar Roberts is the president and chief executive officer of Fidelity Bank of Florida. He began his banking career as a part-time teller while attending college and became a bank president at the age of 29. He has held that position in six Florida banks and served as president of the Florida Bankers Association.

REMEMBERING HOW TO WIN FRIENDS
AND INFLUENCE PEOPLE

In the world of business, we encounter many clients and employees along the way. Something that has been helpful to me, not only in the professional sector but also in my personal life, is Dale Carnegie's book, "How to Win Friends and Influence People." Debuting in 1936, the book was ranked 19th on Time Magazine's "100 Best Books of All Time" list in 2011. Over 30 million copies have been sold. In addition, the information has been used to create the curriculum for Dale Carnegie Training, a leadership course taught in more than 90 countries and 30 languages.

In the book, Carnegie recommends many principles to win friends and influence people. His training course teaches a technique known as "ordered association," whereby memory pictures are created along with an associated principle. Fashioning mental pictures (association) with numbers, rhyming words and action pictures improves a person's ability to remember the important information.

Here are the mental pictures I learned for the first 10 principles of "How to Win Friends and Influence People."

One – Run: The Three C's
Imagine a white horse running across a pasture; the remembered principle is hanging from the horse's saddle horn. It is the three C's – never criticize, condemn or complain.

Two – Zoo: Honest and Sincere Appreciation
A monkey is throwing the principle you are trying to remember at you while you stand in front of its cage. You may imagine a mental picture of you giving a monkey a banana, and it is showing appreciation for it by throwing you a bouquet of flowers. Carnegie's principles include showing honest and sincere appreciation to others.

Three – Tree: An Eager Want
Tied to the top of a very tall tree is the principle you are trying to remember. It is a wanted poster reminding us to arouse in others an eager want.

"While all of these principles are appropriate in various situations, one resonates with me the most. It is to never criticize, condemn or complain."

Four – Door: Genuine Interest
This mental picture is a revolving door that is stuck by a bag of money. As money earns interest, this reminds us to become genuinely interested in other people.

Five – Hive: Always Smile
Coming out of a beehive is a smiling Cheshire cat. The principle for this mental picture reminds us to always smile.

Six – Sick: Called By Name
Picture a rolling hospital gurney with a nameplate on it. This serves as a reminder to follow Carnegie's sixth principle when interacting with others — call them by name. Remember that a person's name is the sweetest and most important sound in any language.

Seven – Heaven: Listening
Envision a stairway to heaven with an ear tumbling down it. This reminds us to be good listeners. Encourage others to talk about themselves.

Eight – Gate: Speak Of Interest
Imagine a swinging gate with a set of false teeth attached to it as it swings back and forth. This reminds us of Carnegie's principle to talk in terms of other people's interests.

Nine – Wine: Feel Important
There is a crate of wine being unloaded onto a dock. The crate is marked "Imported." This word is utilized to remember Carnegie's principle to make others feel important and to do it sincerely.

10 – Den: Avoid Arguing
Envision a lion in a den growling at you. This is to remind you of Carnegie's principle to avoid arguing. The only way to get the best of an argument is to avoid it.

While all of these principles are appropriate in various situations, one resonates with me the most. It is to never criticize, condemn or complain. No one enjoys a business or personal relationship with someone who is always negative.

"How to Win Friends and Influence People" is a timeless work that still helps many, including myself. I find it interesting that I learned these rules using this memory system nearly four decades ago while attending a Dale Carnegie course. By placing these 10 principles alongside this rhyming scheme, we can remember them and live more productive and successful lives. A few famous and successful people who are graduates of the Dale Carnegie course include: Chuck Norris, Orville Redenbacher, Dave Thomas (Wendy's founder), Zig Ziglar, Lee Iacocca, Warren Buffett and my wife. •

BEST PRACTICES

PERSONAL WELLNESS

J. Lamar ROBERTS

MY FORMULA FOR HEALTH, HAPPINESS AND SUCCESS
(D+B) X (G+F) X (P+P+P)P − HHS

Health, Happiness and Success (HHS) are three of the most important aspects of my life, and everyone else's for that matter. Over the years, I have identified several important factors that have helped me achieve HHS. This article was written to share my definition of these goals and the steps I have taken to accomplish them.

HEALTH: To me, a healthy life is one in which a person lives to life expectancy without disease or physical compromise. Being healthy requires planning and discipline in order to control weight, blood pressure, and normal blood measurements. Exercise, as well as physical exams by a physician, must also be part of the plan. Our health has more to do with the daily choices we make and how we live our lives than the occasional visit to the doctor, though the visits provide essential feedback on our current condition.

HAPPINESS: Walt Disney said, "Happiness is a state of mind. It's just according to the way you look at things." I believe most of us are about as happy as we allow ourselves to be. In order to be happy, we need something to do, something to look forward to and someone to love. I am fortunate to have all three. Most unhappy people have a negative outlook on life, are faultfinders and blame others for their problems. Also, they are usually missing one or more of the three needs mentioned above.

SUCCESS: Success is "the progressive realization of worthy goals." It can be measured by where people are currently compared to where they were when they established their goals. I started my banking career as a part-time teller while attending college. My goal was to become an executive and by age 29, I was elected president of a Florida bank. Each year I set new or different goals for various aspects of my life.

My Formula

The next formulas refer to steps that you can do to achieve HHS. They are cumulative and ongoing throughout a person's life.

(D+B) DISCIPLINE + BALANCE: We must be self-disciplined to avoid negative consequences. This applies to many aspects of life such as wellness, relationships, and career. When we spend too little or too much time on any of these areas, we will have an unbalanced situation. This is not to say there are times when one area needs more attention than others, but we should always keep all the "balls in the air."

(G + F) GOALS + FOCUS: Often what becomes a goal begins as a dream. However, dreams, wishes or wants seldom accomplish our objectives unless specific goals are set. Goals should be understandable, achievable and measurable. The measurements should always include time and either dollars, numbers or percentages. Goals will not be met unless the person setting them focuses on them. I suggest that goals be reviewed monthly or quarterly.

(P + P + P) PLAN + PATIENCE + PERSISTENCE: My mother told me to "plan my work and then work my plan." Goals without focus or a plan without a strategy are probably doomed for failure. Good things, like good wine, take time. Do not give up. What appears to be a failure could simply be a step in the learning process that allows you to realize what you tried did not work and that another approach is necessary. Often a setback is a set up for a comeback so be patient and persistent with your plan.

Master Planner

You will notice the three P's portion of the formula is raised to the "P" power. This refers to a higher power, which is God for me. The "P" is also for prayer and, of course, prayer is talking to God; praising, thanking and listening to Him, as well as asking Him for what you want for others and need for yourself. It should also include "Let Thero will be done," because I believe He is the Master Planner. The Serenity Prayer is one of my favorites, and a copy of it is framed on my office credenza. It says: God, grant me the serenity to accept the things I cannot change, courage to change the things I can, and wisdom to know the difference.

Change is an important part of being Happy, Healthy and Successful. Most people do not like to change; they just want others to change to make things better. However, nothing improves until something changes, and that may often be ourselves.

| BEST PRACTICES

J. Lamar **ROBERTS**

THE VOWELS OF SUCCESS
CHARACTERISTICS THAT SHAPE YOUR FUTURE

> Believe it or not, the loudest voice you hear is your own. It can work for or against you, depending on the message.

Every person defines the characteristics of success differently and, while each definition is unique, there are some fundamentals that run true through each of them. These characteristics and traits have been touched on and dissected over the years by well-known authors like Zig Ziglar, Dr. Robert H. Schuller, Dr. Norman Vincent Peale and Napoleon Hill, to contemporary authors that will one day be equally familiar to us. However, to sum up the pages of all of these beautifully written manuscripts, below are The Vowels of Success as a quick reference on what characteristics one must have in order to be successful in life and in business.

ATTITUDE, APTITUDE, ALTITUDE
Attitude is more important than *aptitude* in determining your *altitude*. You must have a positive outlook on life and people. The absence of negative thinking in your life and/or business is imperative. You may have heard it referenced as "stinkin' thinkin'" or getting a "check up from the neck up for hardening of your attitude." The positive attitude you have towards any given situation greatly impacts its outcome. Remember; always think positively... it is contagious and it achieves positive results.

ENTHUSIASM, EDUCATION, EXPERIENCE
Enthusiasm coupled with *education* and *experience* can take you to new heights. You can have all of the degrees, accreditations and certifications in the world, but without *enthusiasm*, you have little. Always be excited about learning and doing. This combination will lead to success.

IMPORTANT, INVOLVED, INFORMED
It is *important* to make others feel important. You can accomplish that by getting those around you *involved* and keeping them *informed*. Employees or colleagues feel important when their opinions are valued and they are kept informed of recent changes in the company. When they feel important, they become better team members.

OPTIMISTIC, OTHERS, OPPORTUNITIES
An *optimistic* mindset gives you a positive approach to challenges. *Others* can be helpful with these challenges, as there is no such thing as a self-made man. If offered help, accept it with open arms. Everyone needs mentors. *optimism* and learning from others will lead to *opportunities*. These opportunities can produce success.

UNIQUE

You are *unique*, having no like or equal. Your parents may have told you "just be yourself." They were right! No one else is like you; you were made in the divine and perfect image of the Creator. Remember that throughout your day – it is a powerful fact.

YOU

Sometimes "Y" is a vowel. In the vowels of success, there is always a "Y". It represents YOU.

It all comes down to YOU! This last vowel takes all of the above and melds them together. To be successful in life and business it takes – your *attitude*, your *enthusiasm*, your ability to make others feel *important*, your *optimism* and your *uniqueness*.

You may have noticed that one of the common denominators within these characteristics is having a PMA -- a positive mental attitude. Believe it or not, the loudest voice you hear is your own. It can work for or against you, depending on the message. You can build yourself up or wear yourself down. Be accountable for your inner conversations so they can propel you towards success.

PERSONALITY PROFILES

For over thirty years, I have used personality profiles to help me hire the right person for the right jobs. These profiles tell employers nothing about a person's education, intelligence, wisdom or even maturity. However, they do indicate the type of work a person would be inclined to enjoy doing and therefore would probably do well. Below are a couple profiles on me.

> *Based on Lamar's responses, the report has selected a general statement to provide a broad understanding of his work style. These statements identify the basic natural behavior that he brings to the job. This is, if left on his own, these statements identify HOW HE WOULD CHOOSE TO DO THE JOB. Use the general characteristic to gain a better understanding of Lamar's natural behavior.*
>
> Lamar is often frustrated when working with others who do not share the same sense of urgency. He wants to be viewed as self-reliant and willing to pay the price for success. He can be aggressive and direct, but still be considerate of people. Other people realize that directness is one of his greatest strengths. He displays a high energy factor and is optimistic about the results he can achieve. The word "can't" is not in his vocabulary. Many people see him as a self-starter dedicated to achieving results. He is deadline conscious and becomes irritated if deadlines are delayed or missed. He is goal-oriented and driven by results. He is the team member who will try to keep the others on task. He is a goal-oriented manager who believes in harnessing people to help him achieve his goals. Lamar prefers an environment with variety and change. He is at his best when many projects are underway at once. He embraces visions not always seen by others. Lamar's creative mind allows him to see the "big picture."
>
> Lamar should realize that at times he needs to think a project through, beginning to end, before starting the project. He is decisive and prefers to work for a decisive manager. He can experience stress if his manager does not possess similar traits. Sometimes he becomes emotionally involved in the decision-making process. He prefers authority equal to his responsibility. Lamar finds it easy to share his opinions on solving work-related problems. He likes to make decisions quickly. He will work long hours until a tough problem is solved. After it is solved, Lamar may become bored with any routine work that follows. Many people see his decision as high-risk decisions. However, after the decision is made, he tends to work hard for a successful outcome.[1]

---

[1] TTI Success Insights, DiSC Survey Report.

General Characteristics Continued

Lamar likes people who give him options as compared to their opinions. The options may help him make decisions, and he values his own opinion over that of others! His creative and active mind may hinder his ability to communicate to others effectively. He may present the information in a form that cannot be easily understood by some people. He may lack the patience to listen and communicate with slower acting people. He likes people who present their case effectively. When they do, he can then make a quicker assessment or decision. Lamar tends to be intolerant of people who seem ambiguous or think too slowly. He may lose interest in what others are saying if they ramble or don't speak to the point. His active mind is already moving ahead. He should exhibit more patience and ask questions to make sure that others have understood what he has said. He challenges people who volunteer their opinions.

Strongest Behaviors

Lamar's PI Pattern is extremely wide, which means that his behaviors are very strongly expressed and his needs are very strongly felt.

Lamar will most strongly express the following behaviors:

- Connecting very quickly to others, he's strongly motivated to build and leverage relationships to get work done. Openly and easily shares information about himself.
- Strikingly expressive, effusive, and verbal in communicating; he talks a lot, and very quickly. Enthusiastically persuades and motivates others by adjusting his message and delivery to the current recipient.
- Very collaborative, he works almost exclusively with and through others. Strong intuitive understanding of team cohesion, dynamics, and interpersonal relations.
- Socially informal, extroverted, and outgoing; gets familiar quickly. Communicates in an uninhibited, lively, and adaptable manner, drawing others into the conversation.
- Interested in people, building relationships, and teamwork rather than technical matters. Affable, optimistic, and easily trusting.
- Focused on goals and the people he needs to get there, not details or plans; frequently delegates details.

Summary

Lamar is an engaging, stimulating communicator, poised and capable of projecting enthusiasm and warmth, and of motivating other people.

He has a strong sense of urgency, initiative and competitive drive to get things done, with emphasis on working with and through people in the process. He understands people well and uses that understanding effectively in influencing and persuading others to act.

Impatient for results and particularly impatient with details and routines, Lamar is a confident and venturesome "doer" and decision-maker who will delegate details and can also delegate responsibility and authority when necessary. Lamar is a self-starter who can also be skillful at training and developing others. He applies pressure for results, but in doing so, his style is more "selling" than "telling".

At ease and self-assured with groups or in making new contacts, Lamar is gregarious and extroverted, has an invigorating impact on people, and is always "selling" in a general sense. He learns and reacts quickly and works at a faster-than-average pace. Able to adapt quickly to change and variety in his work, he will become impatient and less effective if required to work primarily with repetitive routines and details.

In general terms, Lamar is an ambitious and driving person who is motivated by opportunity for advancement to levels of responsibility where he can use his skills as team builder, motivator and mover.

Management Style

As a manager of people or projects, Lamar will be:

- Broadly focused: his attention is on where he's bringing his team, and what goals he wants them to achieve, rather than on the specifics of how they will get there
- Strongly focused on cohesion, communication, morale, and team accomplishment;

he achieves his goals through them and with them
- Comfortable delegating authority; he is eager to discuss his ideas with others is amenable to changing his mind if it helps his overall goal
- At ease in delegating details and implementation plans
- Quick, friendly and broadly-focused when following-up on delegated tasks. he is eager to get details completed quickly, freeing up his team to work on the next objective
- Flexible in working with different kinds of people
- Engaging and enthusiastic – confident in his ability to persuade others towards his point-of-view.

Influencing Style

As an influencer, Lamar will be:

- Confident and persuasive in guiding the process towards his goal
- Eager to keep the process moving along as quickly as possible; utilizes persuasion, not pressure, to gain agreement
- Skillful with the emotional aspects of influencing others; connecting with others more than the specific details of the implementation; leveraging this information to gain agreement quickly
- Adept at navigating the "politics" of an organization; finding the key players and utilizing persuasive talk to gain agreement
- Flexible and adaptable; relying on his ability to think on his feet rather than making a distinct plan to follow
- Better at influencing others about intangibles such as ideas or concepts

Management Strategies

To maximize his effectiveness, productivity, and job satisfaction, consider providing Lamar with the following:

- Opportunities for involvement and interaction with people
- Some independence and flexibility in his activities
- Freedom from repetitive routine and details in work which provides variety and change of pace
- Opportunities to learn and advance at a fairly fast pace
- Recognition and reward for communications and leadership skills demonstrated
- Social and status recognition as rewards for achievement.

RESUME

J. Lamar Roberts

EMPLOYMENT:

President and CEO of six Florida banks and Chairman of the board of a seventh since 1971 (Three became high performing banks, two were "turn around" situations and three were crisis management challenges.)

Fidelity Bank of Florida, N.A.
    Merritt Island, FL-President & CEO, 2012-2019

First National Bank of Central Florida
    Winter Park, FL – President, 2009 - 2011

First National Bank of Pasco
    Dade City, FL – President & CEO, 1992 - 2009

The American Bank of the South
    Merritt Island, FL – Executive Vice President, 1991 - 1992

First National Bank & Trust
    Fort Walton Beach, FL – President & CEO, 1981 - 1991

Florida National Bank of Brevard
    Titusville, FL – President & CEO, 1979 - 1981

Dixie County State Bank
    Cross City, FL – President & CEO, 1971 - 1979

EDUCATION:

FORMAL: Georgia State University, Atlanta, Georgia 1960 – 1964
                  West Georgia College, Carrollton, Georgia 1959 – 1960

BANKING: Graduate School of Bank Investments, University of Oklahoma, 1982
                  National Commercial Lending Graduate School, Univ. of Oklahoma, 1980
                  Graduate School of Banking of the South, Louisiana State Univ., 1966-1968
                  Georgia Banking School, University of Georgia, 1962-1964

PROFESSIONAL DESIGNATIONS:
                  American Bankers Association, Certified Commercial Lender (CCL)
                  Institute of Certified Bankers, Certified Lender-Business Banking (CLBB)

PRESENTATIONS GIVEN:

Panel Member, BAI Bank President's Forum – *"High-Performance Banking"*

Florida Independent Bankers Convention – *"High-Performance Banking"*

Florida Bankers Association Convention – *"High-Performance Banking"*

ABA/BMA Community Bankers Conference – *"Incentive Pay"*

Arkansas Association of Bank Holding Companies – *"Business Development and Incentive Compensation"*

Florida School of Banking at University of Florida – *"Bank Management and Leadership"*

University of Wisconsin – Graduate School of Banking Lecturer – *"Developing a Sales Culture"*

National Bank of Commerce Investment Seminar – *"Future of Community Banking"*

Congressional Sub-committee Testimony – *"Banking on Retirement Security: A Guaranteed Rate of Return"*

Florida Bank President's Summit – *"What Keeps Bankers Awake at Night"*

FLORIDA BANKERS ASSOCIATION INVOLVEMENT:

Director, Florida Bankers Association Branch Management Institute (2 Years)

Director & Instructor, Florida School of Banking (5 Years)

Chairman, Florida Bankers Association Education Council

Member, Florida Bankers Association Board of Directors

Chairman, Florida Bankers Association Directors Executive Committee

Chairman, Florida Bankers Association Tier 1 Directors

President, Florida Bankers Association 2004 - 2005

OTHER INDUSTRY INVOLVEMENT:

Member, American Bankers Association Community Bankers Council

Member, ABA Community Bankers Council Executive Committee

Director, Independent Community Bankers of America (Representing Florida)

Director, ICBA Mortgage Corporation

Member, ICBA Executive Committee (Director At Large) only two for the USA

Chairman, Independent Bankers' Bank of Florida

Chairman, Florida Bankers Insurance Trust

Strategic Planning Facilitator for several Banks

OTHER LEADERSHIP POSITIONS:

City Council President

Mayor and Municipal Judge

Director, Housing Authority (Appointed by the Governor)

Director, River Authority (Appointed by the Governor)

Vice President, of two Community College Foundations

Chairman, Hospital Board of Trustees

President, Committee of 100

President, of two Chambers of Commerce

President, Habitat for Humanity Affiliate

Citizen of the Year – Zephyrhills, Florida

Business Leader of the Year – Dade City, Florida

J. Lamar Roberts

Summary

Mr. Roberts has served as President, CEO or Chairman of six Florida banks. Known equally for his leadership with top-performing, as well as 'turnaround' banks, he understands the ever-increasing regulatory pressures faced by his peers.

As a veteran Florida community bank executive, Roberts was first elected bank President at age 29 During his extensive career, he led three banks to become the first or second top performers in the state, and oversaw four "turnarounds" including confronting and managing Memorandum of Understandings, Formal Agreements and Cease and Decease mandates. His career included leading two distressed banks to top performance, and nursing another through a regulatory closing.

His leadership skills, knowledge, and experience have been extensively utilized by his community bank peers. He served as President of the Florida Bankers Association, on the Executive Committee of the Community Banker's Council of the American Bankers Association and as a Director and member of the Executive Committee of the Independent Community Bankers Association. He was elected Chairman of the Board of the Florida Independent Bankers Bank as well as Chairman of the Board of the Florida Bankers Insurance Trust. He has been a guest lecturer for the Florida School of Banking at the University of Florida and for the Graduate Banking School at the University of Wisconsin.

His leadership service extends deep into the community, having taken leadership roles in government, civic, education, banking, and religious organizations. These include being elected mayor, municipal judge and city council president. He has also been President of a Rotary Club, two Chambers of Commerce and an economic development organization. He and his wife, Cindy, are proud of being two of the founders of one of the country's most successful Habitat for Humanity affiliates. He was also an organizer of the Okaloosa-Walton Community College Foundation, which now has assets exceeding $51,000,000.

BUSINESS CARDS I HAD OVER MY CAREER.

J. LAMAR ROBERTS
VICE PRESIDENT & CASHIER
DIXIE COUNTY STATE BANK
CROSS CITY, FLORIDA
TEL: 498-3367

LAMAR ROBERTS
ASSISTANT CASHIER
THE MANUFACTURERS NATIONAL BANK
NEWNAN, GEORGIA

TITUSVILLE (305) 267-1694
MELBOURNE (305) 725-9000
LAMAR ROBERTS
PRESIDENT
FLORIDA NATIONAL BANK OF BREVARD COUNTY
P. O. BOX 5619 / 922 CHENEY HIGHWAY / TITUSVILLE, FLORIDA 32780
27 EAST HIBISCUS / MELBOURNE, FLORIDA 32901

J. LAMAR ROBERTS
PRESIDENT
DIXIE COUNTY STATE BANK
CROSS CITY, FLORIDA 32628
PHONE: 498-3367

1st FIRST NATIONAL BANK
OF OKALOOSA COUNTY

J. LAMAR ROBERTS, CCL
PRESIDENT AND CEO

99 EGLIN PARKWAY • P.O. DRAWER 1207   AREA CODE 904
FORT WALTON BEACH, FLORIDA 32549   PHONE 243-7511

THE AMERICAN BANK
OF THE SOUTH

J. LAMAR ROBERTS
Executive Vice President

P.O. Box 540548
TELEPHONE (407) 452-5480
Merritt Island, FL 32954-0548

First National
BANK OF CENTRAL FLORIDA

J. Lamar Roberts
President

388 North New York Avenue • Winter Park, Florida 32789
Office: 407-539-7729 • Fax: 407-622-0766
lroberts@fnbcfla.com • www.BelieveInYourBank.com

 **RMPI CONSULTING**

J. Lamar Roberts

Risk Management & Process Improvement Specialists

Fidelity Bank
OF FLORIDA

1380 N. Courtenay Parkway
Merritt Island, FL 32953
Phone: 321-328-1414
Fax: 321-452-0233

J. Lamar Roberts
President and CEO

lroberts@fbfna.com

www.fbfna.com

GENEALOGY

The genealogy below, prepared by my mother in 1983, is included in the first book she wrote, *Experiences That Live*. It is a story of her life.

She wrote a second book in 1988, titled Precious Children, Ours and Others

```
                           - GENEAOLOGY -
                           -  ROBERTS  -

Lewis M. Roberts,      Born                Deceased
Antionette Phillips,   Born                Deceased
Lewis M. Roberts and Antionette Phillips were married August 20, 1868
Born to this union were nine children -
Lenora, Rena, Annie Bell, Ella Merl, Dee Witt, Albert L., Roscoe V.,
Alverta and Wyatt S. -
Dee Witt Roberts, Born July 29, 1873
     Deceased August 31, 1949
Carrie Catherine Deal, Born August 8, 1879
     Deceased March 3, 1923
Dee Witt Roberts and Carrie Catherine Deal were married November 22, 1899
Born to this union were four children -
John, Paul, Elihu Dee, Johnnie Dee, and Bobbie Lee.


                           - THOMPSON -

Joseph Lewis Thompson, Born November 17, 1858
     Deceased September 2, 1934
Mary Kansas Hammond, Born March 24, 1860
     Deceased December 4, 1955
Joseph Lewis Thompson and Mary Kansas Hammond were married February
1, 1880
Born to this union were nine children -
Three boys and six girls.
Ollie, Annie, Lonnie, Lucy, Ida Lee, Kay, Ebb, Josie and Carrie.


                           - PARHAM -

James Henry Parham, Born September 11, 1860
     Deceased January 26, 1938
Ada Jackson Parnham, Born October 20, 1863
     Deceased August 2, 1947
Born to this union were eleven children -
Ten girls and one boy.
Mary, Ollie, Davie, Grovie, Rosie, Baby (still-birth, not named), Nora,
Robert, Maude, Edna, Winnie.


                        - THOMPSON-PARHAM -

Lonnie Upson Thompson, Born January 28, 1884
     Deceased September 1, 1962
Rosie Roberts Parham, Born March 21, 1893
     Deceased August 20, 1978
Lonnie Thompson and Rosie Parham were married December 25, 1909
Born to this union were four children -
Two boys and two girls.
J. D., Edna, Norene, Harvey.
```

- ROBERTS-THOMPSON -

Elihu Dee Roberts and Edna Thompson were married April 28, 1934.
Born to this union were three children, all boys.
Lonnie Dee Roberts, Born September 26, 1935
Jerry Lamar Roberts, Born July 21, 1941
William Eugene Roberts, Born June 15, 1944

- GRANDCHILDREN -

Bert Alexander Roberts, Born February 22, 1956
Weston Lamar Roberts, Born January 19, 1968
Camille Ann Roberts, Born November 15, 1968
Carla Ann Roberts, Born January 16, 1975
Jay Lamar Roberts, Born November 8, 1981

Elihu Dee Roberts, my Father, died in 1972 in Newnan, GA, age 65

Edna Thompson Roberts, my Mother died in 1998 in Tallahassee, FL, age 86

Lonnie Dee Roberts, my Brother, died in 2001 in Tallahassee, FL, age 66

William (Bill) Roberts, my Brother died in 2016 in Warner Robins, age 71

23 **Top left**, Lonnie and Rosie Thompson, my Mother's parents. The picture was taken in 1913, one year after my mother was born. They lived in Heard County, Georgia near the county seat of Franklin. **Top right**, Jim and Ada Parham, my Mother's grandparents, the picture was taken in 1930 in Heard County, Georgia. **Bottom left**, my Father's parents, Dewitt William Roberts, age 36, and his mother Carrie Catherine Deal Roberts, age 30, his brother, John Paul Roberts, age 3 and my Father in his mother's arms, Elihu Dee Roberts, age 1. The picture was at Rye River Springs near Sarasota, FL, in 1908. **Bottom middle**, my grandfather Thompson's mother, Mary Kansas Hammond Thompson. This picture was taken in 1950. She was born, March 24, 1860, in Heard County, GA. This was thirteen months before the Civil War began. She died at age 95, in 1955, when I was fourteen years old.\. She told me she had heard about the Civil War and Atlanta being burned by Sherman, but they lived about forty miles south of Sherman's march through Georgia. **Bottom right**, my Mother's parents, Lonnie and Rosie Thompson. This picture was taken in 1962, the year before my Grandfather died. They were living in Grantville, Georgia at that time

MY FAVORITE CHRISTIAN ACRONYMS

ASAP	Always Say A Prayer
BIBLE	Basic Instructions Before Leaving Earth
CROSS	Christ Rose on Sacred Sunday
FAITH	Forsaking All, I Trust Him
GRACE	God's Riches At Christ Expense
HOPE	Hang On Praying Expectantly
JOY	Jesus first, Others second, Yourself last
LIFE	Living In Faith Everyday
MAGIC	Mercy and Grace In Christ
NOW	No Opportunity Wasted
OWL	One With the Lord
PUSH	Pray Until Something Happens
STAND	Simply Trust and Never Doubt
TGIF	Thank God I'm Forgiven
WAIT	Wisdom and Answers In Time

SOME OF MY FAVORITE BIBLE VERSES

Hebrews 11:1 (NASB) *Now faith is the assurance of things hoped for, the conviction of things not seen.*

1 Corinthians 13:13 (NIV) *And now these three remain: faith, hope and love. But the greatest of these is love.*

John 3:16 (NASB) *For God so loved the world, that He gave His only begotten Son, that whoever believes in Him shall not perish, but have eternal life.*

John 3:17 (NASB) *For God did not send the Son into the world to judge the world, but that the world might be saved through Him.*

Philippians 4:13 (NIV) *I can do all this through Him who gives me strength.*

John 14:6 (NIV) *Jesus answered, "I am the way and the truth and the life. No one comes to the Father except through me."*

Romans 8:28 (NASB) *And we know that God causes all things to work together for good to those who love God, to those who are called according to His purpose.*

Philippians 4:6 (NASB) *Be anxious for nothing, but in everything by prayer and supplication with thanksgiving let your request be made known to God.*

Acts 16:31 (NASB, emphasis mine) *"Believe in the **Lord Jesus**, and you **will be saved** - you and your household."*

John 15:7 (NASB) *If you abide in Me, and My words abide in you, ask whatever you wish, and it will be done for you.*

Luke 6:15 (NASB) *Do not judge, and you will not be judged; and do not condemn, and you will not be condemned; pardon, and you will be pardoned.*

***Matthew 6:14-15* (GNT)** *If you forgive others the wrongs they have done to you, your Father in heaven will also forgive you. But if you do not forgive others, then your Father will not forgive the wrongs you have done.*

John 14:3 (NIV) *And If I go and prepare a place for you, I will come back and take you to be with me that you also may be where I am.*

SOME OF MY FAVORITE QUOTES

Man. Because he sacrifices his health in order to make money. Then he sacrifices money to recuperate his health. And then he is so anxious about the future that he does not enjoy the present; the result being that he does not live in the present or the future; he lives as if he is never going to die, and then dies having never really lived.
The Dalai Lama
when asked what surprised him most about humanity

"You cannot legislate the poor into freedom by legislating the wealthy out of freedom. What one person receives without working for, another person must work for without receiving. The government cannot give to anybody anything that the government does not first take from somebody else. When half of the people get the idea that they do not have to work because the other half is going to take care of them, and when the other half gets the idea that it does no good to work because somebody else is going to get what they work for, that my dear friend, is about the end of any nation. You cannot multiply wealth by dividing it."
Adrian Rogers

The only thing we have to fear is fear itself.
Franklin D. Roosevelt

Whether you think you can or think you cannot - you're right.
Henry Ford

It is not whether you get knocked down; it's whether you get up.
Coach Vince Lombardi

Faith is not believing that God can, but that God will.
Abraham Lincoln

The secret of success is to find a need and fill it, to find a hurt and heal it, to find somebody with a problem and offer to help solve it.
Dr. Robert H. Schuller

The first and best victory is to conquer self.
Plato

Five Simple Rules for Happiness:
1. Free your heart from hatred.
2. Free your mind from worries.
3. Live simply.
4. Give more.
5. Expect less.
Dr. Norman Vincent Peale

Happiness is simply:

Having something to do,
Something to look forward to and
Someone to love.
Rita Mae Brown

SOME OF MY FAVORITE SONGS

The Hallelujah Chorus

Handel, George Frideric. *Messiah*. Scriptural text compiled by Charles Jennens (1741)

My Way

Paul Anka, lyrics, and Jacques Revaux, composer (1969).

Recorded by Frank Sinatra, Reprise, 1969.

Amazing Grace

Newton, John (text). *Olney Hymns*. (1779)

The Impossible Dream (The Quest)

Mitch Leigh, composer and Joe Darion, lyrics. *Man of La Mancha* (1965).

Recorded by many artists including Frank Sinatra (1966), Jim Nabors (1966), The Temptations (1967), The Smothers Brothers (1968), Elvis Presley (1972), and Luther Vandross (1994)

Near To the Heart of God

Cleland Boyd McAfee (1903)

How Great Thou Art

Carl Gustav Boberg and Stuart K. Hine, translator (1949)

The Lord's Prayer

Traditional liturgical text; based on Luke 11:2-4 and Matt 6:9-13

ACTIVITIES, INVOLVEMENTS, INTEREST I HAVE HAD DURING MY LIFE

They each lasted an average of ten years. Obviously, many overlapped.

- Involvement in Church Music leadership
- Attending colleges and banking schools (12 years)
- Local politics; I ran five races and won three of them
- Hunting and fishing
- Owning and flying an airplane
- Water-skiing and snow skiing
- Horseback riding, Western and English, including jumping rails
- Banking industry leadership roles with the American Banking Association. Independent Community Bankers Association and the Florida Bankers Association
- Habitat for Humanity, founder of a local affiliate, director and president
- Chambers of Commerce President (2) and Economic Development Agency (2), President of one and Vice President of another.
- Military Affairs Committee
- Golf
- Tennis
- Traveled to over 20 foreign countries

www.ingramcontent.com/pod-product-compliance
Lightning Source LLC
LaVergne TN
LVHW041544070426
835507LV00011B/925